WOMEN'S POETRY OF THE 1930s

This comprehensive and beautifully edited volume is a remarkable collection of poems by women who wrote in the interwar years. Much is known about the so-called 'Auden generation', but until now little of women's poetry from this era of rapidly changing gender roles, social values and world politics has been collected or acknowledged. Jane Dowson redresses the balance by gathering together these richly varied poems, many of which were previously out of print, uncollected or simply neglected through time.

Jane Dowson provides an essential framework to the poems with an extensive critical introduction and individual biographies of each poet. This unique anthology sheds a whole new light on women's place in this era of British literary history and demands a reassessment of our understanding of 1930s poetry.

Women's Poetry of the 1930s will be an invaluable resource and a treasured volume for students, scholars and poetry lovers alike.

Jane Dowson is Senior Lecturer in English and Cultural Studies at De Montfort University, Bedford. She has written extensively on the subject of women's poetry.

WOMEN'S POETRY OF THE 1930s

A critical anthology

Edited by Jane Dowson

LONDON AND NEW YORK

First published 1996
by Routledge
11 New Fetter Lane, London EC4P 4EE

Simultaneously published in the USA and Canada
by Routledge
29 West 35th Street, New York, NY 10001

Introduction and editorial material © 1996 Jane Dowson

This collection © 1996 Routledge

Typeset in Janson by Datix International Limited, Bungay, Suffolk

Printed and bound in Great Britain by Clays Ltd, St Ives plc

British Library Cataloguing in Publication Data

A catalogue record for this book is available from the British Library

Library of Congress Cataloguing in Publication Data

Women's Poetry of the 1930s : A critical anthology / edited by Jane
Dowson.
p. cm.
Includes bibliographical references (p.   ).
1. English poetry--Women authors.   2. English poetry--20th
century.   3. Women--Poetry.   I. Dowson, Jane, 1995- .
PR1177.W668   1995
821'.9120809287--dc20   95-14810

ISBN 0-415-13095-6 (hbk)
ISBN 0-415-13096-4 (pbk)

To the memory of
Margharita Widdows,
my grandmother,
a woman and a writer in the 1930s

Into the Whirlwind

A DOCUMENTARY, SUGGESTED BY EUGENIA GINZBURG'S BOOK

Here the peaceful flocks are grazing
    Over the green hill;
Lovers lie on a curly fleece;
    Wind wails and is still.
Now the sirens wail, and cease.
Europe trembles, but the siren
    Only called in fun.

And here the nightmare dread comes true:
    Torn from the fireside, whirled
Into the storm, to meet no more,
    Husband, lover, child,
In cell or camp, year upon year,
Now prove how Soviet tyranny
    Outdoes the cruel Tsar.

Those were the 'thirties. Growing in England knew
The common injocundities, the common
Tremors of adolescence, with its fear
To be found out, found wanting, never to be loved.
Surrounding us were the workless, mortified,
Shaming our youthful dilettante distress,
As now her chronicle of torment shames me.
All of us fearing war . . .

                    Fears were not liars,
For the day came when the sirens wailed in earnest;
Terror broke from the sky, as we knew it must.
A world ended.

                    And a world survived.

Now, as men creep from their holes, what hope
Lifts a faint arc, where the political prisoners
Toil from dark to dark, the deadlong day?
They live in the habitual present tense of pain:
Hope were a span too long to measure, only
Endurance counts, to survive until day ends;
To move, not fall; to live, for a crust of bread.
Life here is a stain in the snow from rag-bound feet,
A wisp of breath, faint as the Arctic sun
Too weak to rise, that lies low on the horizon.
How should the prisoner raise
Her heavy heart, whose only comfort is
That 'each day dies with sleep'?

But gentle sleep's a traitor too,
    For sleep renews the cells
To life, and another day's endurance,
    Though the heart rebels
Against its own absurd resilience.
Brothers, under the same sky,
    They suffer; we go free.

For here again the flocks are grazing
    Over the green hill.
What if the Nazi monster died?
    The heirs of Tolstoy still
Must stain the snow with liberal blood.
And still our lovers' peaceful scene
    Is cross-cut with their pain.

Anne Ridler

Contents

CONTENTS

Preface

This anthology is the result of an investigation into the apparent void of women's poetry in the 1930s. In searching through anthologies and surveys I found no mention of women poets, nor any explanation for their absence. I was intrigued for two reasons: I had been convinced by the more recent re-evaluations of the decade which argue that poetic activity was wider than the narrow representations in the two existing anthologies and that there was no homogeneous 'Thirties poetry'; women, however, were not counted among the writers who had been overlooked. The second factor was that in the recovery of poems by women, there have been collections of the First and Second World Wars, but none of the years between. I assumed, therefore, that for some reason, women who were writers were sticking to prose, or that for social or economic reasons few women were writing. I also wondered if there were verses by women which were too amateurish to be considered in terms of poetry and had been dismissed by literary historians.

I started by reading through the journals myself, both the more serious literary periodicals like *New Verse* and *The Criterion,* and the more comprehensive publications such as *The Listener, New Statesman and Nation* and *Time and Tide.* I initially discovered fourteen poets of standing and three whose output was small; I have since come across three more. During this research, I have met many fans of the individual poets and have encountered almost unanimous support for this project. This book is intended to publish poems which were in danger of remaining in obscurity, to recognise the participation of women in the poetic whirlwinds of the 1930s, and to encourage critical debate about the poetry in the hope that it will feature in future discussions about Thirties, modern, or twentieth-century poetry.

Acknowledgements

I am grateful to the poets, publishers, trustees and colleagues who have been generous in their encouragement and help. I would particularly like to thank: the living poets – E.J. Scovell, Anne Ridler and Naomi Mitchison – for enabling me to test out my assumptions about women and poetry in the 1930s; the families, friends and trustees of other poets for providing information or suggestions – Hugh and Adam Cornford and Timothy Rogers, son, grandson and family friend of Frances Cornford; Lois Godfrey, daughter of Naomi Mitchison; James Hepburn, son of Anna Wickham; Charles Causley and Bruce Hunter, literary executors of the estate of Frances Bellerby; David Higham Associates for Edith Sitwell; Paul Berry, literary executor for Winifred Holtby, and Alan J. Clark – representative for the literary board of management for the late Laura Riding – who has been tireless in supplying information. I am also grateful for the advice of John Lucas and Arnold Rattenbury concerning the political work of Sylvia Townsend Warner and Nancy Cunard. The publishers Jocinta Evans (Open University Press), Stephen Stuart-Smith (Enitharmon), Michael Schmidt (Carcanet), Howard Watson (Chatto & Windus), Tragara and Virago Press have been most helpful. I am thankful for the serendipity in all the correspondence and communications with these and others who share an appreciation of individual poets, particularly Catherine Beeston, Frances Spalding and Anne Harvey. Alison Light and Julie Temperley gave invaluable responses to the first draft. At the University of Leicester, I am indebted to Mark Rawlinson for first suggesting that the 1930s might be a fertile field of enquiry, to Steven Earnshaw for sharing his investigations, and most of all to Nick Everett for his support and guidance from beginning to end.

I depended upon the library at the University of Leicester and the Poetry Library at the South Bank for poetry periodicals and collections, the Department of Manuscripts at the British Library and Sussex University Library for the journals and correspondence of Frances Cornford and Virginia Woolf; the University of Edinburgh loaned the thesis by Donald Smith, *Possible Worlds: The Fiction of Naomi Mitchison* (1982). The publication would not have been possible without the initial advice of Isobel Armstrong, the commitment of Talia Rodgers and a research grant from De Montfort University.

Although it is clichéd, it is also true to say that the interest of my family, friends and Mark have been more valued than they will have known.

Permission to reproduce extracts and poems has kindly been granted as follows: Valentine Ackland – Susanna Pinney and Chatto & Windus; Lilian Bowes Lyon – Thompson Quarrell Solicitors and Chatto & Windus; Frances Cornford – Adam and Hugh Cornford; Nancy Cunard – *New Statesman and Society*; Elizabeth Daryush, from *Collected Poems*, 1976 – Carcanet Press Ltd; Winifred Holtby – with the co-operation of Paul Berry; Sylvia Lynd, from *Collected Poems*, 1945, courtesy of Macmillan; Naomi Mitchison – the author; Ruth Pitter – Enitharmon Press; Laura Riding – Alan J. Clark and the Literary Board of Management; Anne Ridler – the author; Vita Sackville-West – Nigel Nicolson; E.J. Scovell, from *Collected Poems*, 1988 – Carcanet Press Ltd; Edith Sitwell – David Higham Associates; Stevie Smith – the estate of Stevie Smith and Virago Press; Sylvia Townsend Warner, from *Collected Poems*, 1982 – Carcanet Press Ltd; Anna Wickham – the estate of Anna Wickham and Virago Press.

I have not been able to find a record of rights concerning the *Collected Poems* of Dorothy Wellesley. I would be pleased to learn of these or if there have been any omissions; in all cases I have tried to trace the sources of permission and copyright, but these have not always been straightforward.

Abbreviations

In the notes, I have used *CP* for *Collected Poems*, *SP* for *Selected Poems*; and *TLS* for the *Times Literary Supplement*.

Introduction

Rationale

According to Virginia Woolf, a sense of change was the identifiable mark of poets of the 1930s:

> Everywhere change; everywhere revolution. In Germany, in Russia, in Italy, in Spain ... The whole of civilisation, of society was changing ... The books were written under the influence of change, under the threat of war ... They had nothing settled to look at; nothing peaceful to remember; nothing certain to come ... they were stung into consciousness – into self-consciousness, into class-consciousness, into the consciousness of things changing, of things falling, of death perhaps about to come.[1]

The 1930s continue to hold a fascination as a decade in which everyday experience was lived under the shadow of national upheavals – news of events in Europe, the rapid advances in technology and the changes in gender roles and legislation which followed the First World War when women had assumed a new significance as a workforce. The knock-on effect of these developments aroused both anxiety and excitement in the British people. The increased application of electrical power meant shorter working hours and unemployment; at the same time, it provided new employment possibilities, labour-saving gadgets and leisure opportunities. The radio merged the public with the private as the outside world was experienced in the living room. This dissolving of distinctions between the exterior and interior of the home was complemented by the increasing opportunities for women to work, at least in the south of England, and the availability of electric appliances such as the toaster, the iron and the vacuum cleaner meant that there was less 'women's work' to be done. Altogether, there was a blurring of traditional boundaries between the conventional male and female spheres.

Changes in the family unit were both cause and effect of changes in the social order:

> Whether we like it or not, the old family life is changing just as are so many other things. And while we sometimes speak of the good old days, that is only because we are comfortably far away from them.
>
> (Ellen Wilkinson MP)[2]

Ellen Wilkinson was expressing the mixed feelings which characterise this period; 'modern' was an explosive word between the wars and the 1930s need to be understood as a period of contradictory responses, ideological cross-currents and contrasts: 'how unclassifiably various life was. Wretched poverty faced outrageous privilege, and there was a ferment of questions and rejections over society's received ideas by a generation just too young to have taken part in the war.'[3] It is not, however, a simple matter of a generation gap; social differences were entrenched by the disparity between those who did and those who did not benefit from the new prosperity and accentuated the north/south divide. Images of depression and unemployment belong mainly to areas of the north where pits closed; meanwhile, factories opened in the south where the newly waged cultivated their homes and gardens and enjoyed weekly outings to the pictures and the seaside. For the prosperous, the awareness of privilege was often accompanied by guilt, and although leisure time and new pursuits were welcomed, they were at odds with an inherited work ethic and memories of the extreme conditions and hardship of wartime. The fact that in 1931 the Labour and Liberal parties were replaced by the National Government complicates the dominant mythologies of left-wing agitation, hunger marches and support for the Republicans in the Spanish Civil War. Also, Britain in 1930 was quite different from Britain at the end of the decade, by which time the rise of Fascism had deadened the idealisms of the post-war generation and the majority of intellectuals had allegiances with both the political right and with the left. Over-simplistic discussions have belied the complexities and contrasts which inevitably inform the writing of the period; the mixture of styles, such as is evident in the architecture, which created both art deco and Tudor-bethan buildings, or in the visual arts, which experimented with both Surrealism and photographic naturalism, is also evident in the poetry; T.S. Eliot alluded to the rapid development and diversity of styles which he attributed to the 'acceleration of change ... in a bewildered world'.[4]

There is a tension between reinforcing and resisting the concept of a decade when it is the periodising impulse – in its insistence on 'groups' and 'movements' – which is often responsible for excluding women. As this is the first comprehensive exploration of women's poetry during this period, I shall refer to orthodox accounts of Thirties poetry in order to challenge them. The years 1930–39 are taken as a historically specific framework in order to question the misleadingly narrow representation of one group of poets – a Thirties generation of young men aged about thirty, joined by a common zeal to use poetry as a political loud hailer; this myth was partly instigated by the protagonists themselves, some of whom have since discredited it. The later writings of Julian Symons and Stephen Spender, for example, support the argument for a more comprehensive and complex understanding of Thirties poetry.[5] The myth has also partly been established by the two anthologies which have largely influenced our understanding of Thirties poets, and which contain only three poems by a woman.[6] I hope, therefore, that these poems can become integrated into the continuing revision of the dominant images of the Thirties and revitalise discussions of its poetry.

During my investigations into poetry publications of the 1930s, I discovered that women were, in fact, writing and publishing poetry to a remarkable extent, but that they were not treated seriously in critical reviews. I therefore decided to combine poetry with criticism in order to redress this negligence and to extend the perspectives both of the decade and of women's poetry. My aim in segregating poems by women is, by means of their collective impact, to ensure their position in subsequent discussions of the 1930s and to draw attention to individual poets whose work has been erratically represented since the decade; much of it is out of print and some uncollected poems have never been published outside of the original periodicals. All the poets have received niggardly treatment, if any, within literature's critical heritage and have rarely been included in any conspectus of poetic activity in the 1930s.

There are a number of reasons for confining this anthology to women, Britain and the 1930s. This collection fits into the recovery of poetry by women – there have been new volumes of women's poetry of the previous three centuries, of the First and Second World Wars, but not of the intervening years. Although it is true that the poetry of the entire interwar years has been presented almost exclusively in male terms, it is the work of the 1930s in particular which has greatly influenced modern poetry and it is a more powerful concept in British literary history than in Europe or America. Individually, the poets in this anthology have not invariably been included in recent reference guides to women writers or collections of twentieth-century women's poetry. Whether a reader's commitment is to segregation or to integration, a grouping by gender keeps alive the debates about the desirability and possibility of a separate tradition of women's poetry. Such a tradition means that the poems can operate as cultural representations of women's experiences and as transhistorical texts which connect to poetry by women across chronological or cultural divides. As with all anthologies, this one should also provide an introduction to the poets included and encourage enquiry into their larger oeuvres. I have necessarily chosen poems which originate in the 1930s; consequently, they may represent a particular stage in the evolution of a poet's writing; in the individual introductions I have attempted to discuss the poems in this selection and then to indicate the range and characteristics of the poetry more generally and refer to critical commentaries, where they exist, as a starting point for further discussion.

To qualify for inclusion within the anthology, a poet must have had at least one collection of her own published – in most cases there were many more than one. For the purposes of reassessing the established concepts of the decade in Britain, the poets are British, with the exception of Laura Riding, whose residence, extensive activities and influence in England deserve acknowledgement. Her poems, however, cannot be included in a woman-only volume, in respect of her wishes. Kathleen Raine has also prohibited the reproduction of her early poems but is discussed for her successful publishing achievements during the period. I have similarly included a profile, but no poems, for Frances Bellerby in order to register her presence even though it is difficult to determine whether any of her poems were actually written during these 'lost years' of personal crisis.

Delimitation by the decade was particularly difficult with poetry by women; although in many cases, dates of writing and publication were nearly simultaneous, in others, the interim was considerable. Stevie Smith, for example, wrote literally hundreds of poems, many of which were not published until 1981.[7] Similarly, Sylvia Townsend Warner, although close in age, political outlook and technique to W.H. Auden and although she wrote the majority of her poems in the 1930s, did not see them all published. Anna Wickham, whose *Writings* first appeared in 1984, wrote over a thousand poems, but achieved only small publication at the time. I have taken poems which were written or published in a poetry collection for the first time in the 1930s. Occasionally, where a poem has not been dated, it has been included if it appeared in a periodical between 1930 and 1939, on the assumption that it was written in the 1930s or selected for its relevance to the literary climate. I have printed dates where they accompanied the poems or where a poem appears to be previously uncollected.

These are not obscure writers. Stevie Smith is well known for her poetry but has not been connected with the 1930s. Vita Sackville-West, Sylvia Townsend Warner, Naomi Mitchison and Winifred Holtby are more familiar for their prose, although they, like Valentine Ackland, longed for recognition as poets. Laura Riding and Edith Sitwell have reputations as forceful personalities but the poetry itself is seldom debated. Some, such as Frances Cornford, Anne Ridler, Anna Wickham and E.J. Scovell, have always had a discreet but steady following with some moments of greater glory. Dorothy Wellesley, Lilian Bowes Lyon and Elizabeth Daryush, are rarely spoken of now, but these three poets published more collections between 1930 and 1939 than the majority of their male or female contemporaries. Sylvia Lynd and Nancy Cunard made small but significant contributions. I have decided to omit the Scottish writer Olive Fraser (1909–1977) because she did not publish any collections herself although her unusual life and works have posthumously been recorded. Her few poems in the 1930s are from her student days, and to include them would do a disservice to the best work of her later years.[8] Stella Gibbons (1902–1989) considered herself a poet but her success was in her prose, notably, *Cold Comfort Farm* (1932). Although she published three volumes of poetry and a *Collected Poems* (1950), her poems were barely published or reviewed in journals; she has not since been deemed a 'neglected poet', but there may well be scope to reconsider her in this way. One of her poems is included in the *Time and Tide* section.

The uncollected poems from *Time and Tide* are included to signal names of women whose individual poems were often published and to signify the importance of that journal in promoting women as contributors and reviewers. The articles, reviews, correspondence, short stories and poems are evidence of the changing experiences and the dynamic activities of women between the wars, when questions of female identity, status and personal freedoms pertained, of course, to more than half of the population. Many of these poems represent a woman's perspective and centre on a female subject. A continuing preoccupation with sexual politics is evident through reading interwar records and fiction; journals were full of stories, articles and correspondence about the changing expectations of gender roles. *The Listener*, for example, ran a series on 'The Present Crisis of Marriage' which was subtitled 'one of the most debatable questions of our time'.[9]

I have included poems from *The Listener* because poems by women were frequently read on the air and the increasingly widespread influence of the radio has been underestimated. The radio also had the potential to bridge social divides by taking art and literature into homes nationwide. Its preoccupation with 'standards', however, suggests that it also reinforced cultural divisions. I recognise the intersection of class and culture when extending the versions of the period, but I confined my search to literary sources and did not investigate the women's magazines or popular newspapers; I was primarily concerned to demonstrate the involvement of women in literary activities and to demonstrate their successful manipulations of received literary codes.

Having said that, the poets often challenge the dividing line between the literary and the popular. I could also have included a section of poems from the anti-fascist paper *Left Review* in order to emphasise the political commitments of women like Sylvia Townsend Warner, Valentine Ackland, Winifred Holtby, Naomi Mitchison and Nancy Cunard who have often been 'depoliticised' in biographies. Instead, I have incorporated the poems into their respective sections. Additionally, *Left Review* consisted mainly of articles, reviews and some fiction.

I have placed the individual bibliographies in the introductory pages to each poet in order to exhibit the extent of their publications – I have not listed their prose works. In order to encourage interest in the poems, I have kept biographical details to a minimum, but given sufficient sketches to point to the *diversity* of education and occupations and to the varieties and unorthodoxies of their differing personal circumstances. These biographical details indicate the range of personalities, backgrounds and lifestyles; the initiatives and travels are reminders of the new mobility allowed to women with money. Emphasis remains, however, on their professional activities and achievements. The poets' personal lives *are*, undeniably, interesting: there are records of battles with ill health and depression, accidents and suicides – attempted or successful; several rejected marriage and, by choosing independence, experienced family and marital breakdowns; where they publicly engaged in sexual or social politics they often caused scandals by their behaviour or outspoken journalism. These controversies have mostly been well documented in the autobiographical writings and biographies which I have indicated for further reading.

I could have arranged the poets chronologically by birth in order to contest the assumption that age is commensurate with outlook – the oldest, Anna Wickham, is the most overtly radical and the most technically unorthodox, and two of the youngest, E.J. Scovell and Kathleen Raine, are the least tethered to the topical – alphabetical order is, however, more democratic and easy to use. The number of poems selected for each poet is various and is determined by length, the quantity of poetry written, its relevance to the emphasis on change or woman-centred perspectives and the availability of the poetry – I have tried, where appropriate, to privilege poets like Valentine Ackland, Naomi Mitchison and Vita Sackville-West whose work is largely uncollected or out of print. The amount of discussion about each poet is also uneven and, again, determined by the number of poems and the quantity or appropriateness of available information.

This anthology is essentially a statement of the existence of the poetry but the question of its value is, nevertheless, integral to its selection and reception. My own doubts about the worthiness of the poetry were assuaged by *reading* it and realising that the poems had not been weighed and found wanting, but had simply been ignored. I had anticipated that women's poetry, if it existed, must be predominantly domestic and therefore out of sync with a poetry characterised by political awareness and social realism. This was not so. Such a presupposition was fallacious anyway because there is little homogeneity in Thirties poetry nor in poetry by women. There was no more consensus about a 'good poem' than there was similarity between the poets. There are many and complex reasons for the occlusion of women; in literary records, however, I did not find any evidence of considered dismissal of their poetry, but I often found something more akin to what Donald Davie, on discovering Elizabeth Daryush, called 'frivolity, superficiality and cynicism':

> When an unprejudiced literary history of our century comes to be written, our failure to recognise Elizabeth Daryush will be one of the most telling and lamentable charges that can be laid at our door. The cold silence that has prevailed about her work, through one decade after another, is so total that there can be no question of fixing the blame here or there, finding scapegoats. We are *all* at fault, in a way that points therefore to some really deep-seated frivolity, superficiality, cynicism through several generations of readers of English poetry.[10]

The deep-seated resistance to poetry by women is long-standing and perpetual: 'In Britain the tradition that women do not write great poetry is too unconscious and too deep to be easily shifted, even when superficial changes in attitude appear to be occurring.'[11]

Within the broader terms of the decade, women represented the mixed climate, both ideologically and stylistically. In their poems can be perceived the co-existing pressures of the new

demand for both social and psychological realism; they attempted
to be observers, to imitate the patterns of everyday speech and to ˙
represent the compressed simultaneity of the unconscious. Their
styles range from the sonnets and syllabic metres of Elizabeth
Daryush to the lyrics of Anna Wickham, the Elizabethan stanzas
of Sylvia Townsend Warner or the mock-heroics of Ruth Pitter
and there is variety and range within each poet.

Reassessing the 1930s

The literary mythologies of the 'poets of the 1930s', as suggested by
the defining term itself, concern concepts of a generation, a poetic
movement and a decade. Samuel Hynes, in *The Auden Generation*
(1979), identifies the 'generation' as a group born between 1900 and
1914, led by Auden, and with a commitment to left-wing politics.
Such totemism is too tidy and is misleading: accusations of ageism
apart, poetry was not the exclusive property of the young nor was
the division between old and young so clear cut; the atmosphere in
1939 was different from that of 1930; there were several currents of
poetry, and poetry changed during the course of the decade. In
order to establish women within the boundaries of literary discussions, the ground has to be cleared by unsettling these myths of a
Thirties coterie. This volume of poetry by women will not wholly
contradict the alleged influence of the Audenesque, but it must
change and challenge the persistent portrayals of a few cultural
luminaries. Auden and company were undoubtedly *but not exclusively*
significant to the directions of poetry. The act of positioning women
within received versions of literary history challenges the versions
themselves and the processes by which they have been constructed.
It would be dishonest to avoid naming men and male-constructed
critical categories for the sake of substituting one exclusivity for
another. Such mimeticism rather valorises the competitive urge
which has been responsible for the disparagement of women. The
names of critics, poets and familiarised terms are common starting
points from which to explore a more complex and complete world.

When compiling an anthology of the period, the erstwhile
pontifical editor of *New Verse*, Geoffrey Grigson, retrospectively
recognised that the fluidity of poetic practice in the 1930s made it
difficult to identify a 'representative' poem: 'one cannot talk too

much of schools and generations and directions.'[12] Yeats, in his 'National Lecture on Modern Poetry' published in *The Listener*, in 1936, sometimes considered the decade's pivotal year, outlined the various fashions: he acknowledged the 'young influential poets of today', maintained that T.S. Eliot was the most revolutionary poet, although 'stylistically alone', estimated that there was also a greater richness in lyrical poetry than in any previous period since the seventeenth century, and, naturally, paid tribute to the Irish movement, which was growing 'in a different direction'.[13] After 1936, the 'surrealist' poets, although shortlived, were significant, Walter de la Mare regained favour and Dylan Thomas assumed more importance; the second edition of Gerard Manley Hopkins' *Poems* was published in 1930 and his continuing influence is evident in several poets. There was an increasing disassociation of art from politics and by 1940 Cyril Connolly declared the failure of social realism as an aesthetic doctrine.[14]

In the revised version of his classic text *The Thirties: A Dream Revolved* (1960), Julian Symons reflects on the naiveté of his own and others' early over-imaginative representations of the 1930s and, with hindsight, Stephen Spender disputes that there were opposed generations:

> My own Thirties generation – which seems to be identified with Auden, Isherwood, MacNeice, C. Day-Lewis and myself . . . never became so politicised as to disagree seriously with an older generation of writers who held views often described as 'reactionary', fascist even, but whom we admired this side of idolatry: W.B. Yeats, D.H. Lawrence and – most of all – T.S. Eliot.[15]

Spender gives further testimony against the myths of a cohesive group: there was 'no movement . . . no meeting or manifestos' – he, Auden and Day-Lewis were not in the same room until 1948. The perceived commonality of the practices of just a handful of poets has therefore been erroneously used as a measure for all poetry of the period. T.S. Eliot himself noted the impossibility of grouping poets, whether in terms of influence, the poet's aims, a common idiom, vocabulary or metre:

> [they] do not unanimously, or even predominantly, adopt the words and images of an urban, industrialised and mechanised

civilisation; they do not have the same political or religious views, or any political bias or religious conviction at all.[16]

The likenesses and the political commitments have, therefore, been overstated; each poet was different and, for most, any active politics was shortlived. According to Robin Skelton, genuine social action was at odds with the overriding question of the poet's image which was exceptionally important to the men of the Thirties: 'It almost seems as if the main task of many poets was to make an assertion about the poet's function, rather than to perform that function.'[17]

Virginia Woolf explains that it was an awareness of social disparity which complicated the self-perception and role of the artist; it divided the poets from the people whom they sought to represent. The alleged generation gap was, then, less marked than this social divide which presented a dilemma for the writers who realised that their safe towers of privilege were founded upon injustice and tyranny:

> it was wrong for a small class to possess education that other people paid for; wrong to stand upon the gold that a bourgeois father had made from his bourgeois profession. It was wrong; yet how could they make it right?[18]

Nevertheless, the socialism of MacSpaunday[19] was largely intellectualised and born as much out of imagination as of experience. These poets did not need to enter the acquisition race of the suburban street; instead, they used minimalist architecture and the rationalisation of town planning as subject matter for experimentation with post-imagist reductivism and clear concrete forms. They found in the repetitions of production lines and standardised housing welcome material for new rhythms. From high rise flats and factory chimneys they derived an imagery which contrasted to their own prep school playgrounds, public school rugby fields and Oxbridge quads and to the leafy boughs or barbed wires and setting suns of the Georgian or First World War poets. During the first half of the 1930s, the young dream-makers were enervated by the artistic possibilities of oppositions, such as the speed of industrial pioneering versus rural stasis and the Mass Observation movement of 1937 epitomised their role as spectators.[20]

At the same time, these poets experienced genuine guilt and confusion about the relationship between their art and political change. Virginia Woolf created the term 'leaning tower writers' for 'all those writers [who] are acutely tower conscious; conscious of their middle-class birth; of their expensive educations' but who did not want to leave their exalted place within the tower. 'They cannot throw away their education; they cannot throw away their upbringing,'[21] and they realise that they are profiting by a society which they abuse.[22] This sense of the poet as a dweller in two worlds, 'one dying, the other struggling to be born',[23] is the most marked tendency of 'leaning tower' literature, and explains the violence and also the half-heartedness of the poets' attacks upon bourgeois society. This duality also explains the Janus-like nature of much Thirties poetry which is constantly looking to the past and the future.

Virginia Woolf concluded that the poets developed 'the longing to be closer to their kind, to write the common speech of their kind, to share the emotions of their kind, no longer to be isolated and exalted in solitary state upon their tower, but to be down on the ground with the mass of human kind.'[24] In citing Virginia Woolf, I am accepting a version of the 1930s as articulated by the intellectuals. It is true that some of these women poets also colluded with literary culture and were conscious of social privilege. In the frontispiece poem, 'Into the Whirlwind',[25] Anne Ridler alludes to the 'shame' of being surrounded by the 'workless' and Elizabeth Daryush's poem, 'Children of Wealth' can be interpreted as self-accusing. Others, like Stevie Smith, Ruth Pitter, Sylvia Townsend Warner and Frances Cornford do not seem to feel separated from the disadvantaged whom they depict. The difference for all the women was that in spite of their educations or inherited wealth, they had little power. Vita Sackville-West, for example, could not inherit her family home. The women also tended to translate their concerns into social and political activity. Consequently, women could write of injustice without patronising it and often without the guilt or anxiety of male privilege.

In reassessing the received ideas of an identifiable Thirties poetry, it is clear that if there is any *Zeitgeist* it is uncertainty. It is significant, however, that it is the sense of change rather than actual revolution: the inability to make a total break from the past is evident in the pervasive rhetoric and imagery of the First World War and all writers expressed mixed feelings about the turning world. What most unites all the poets, regardless of age or gender, is a preoccupation with finding a language with which to marry the sense of the moment with the sense of tradition. Nevertheless, there was little stylistic conformity and the overriding impression is of diversity. As in the 1990s, editors' interests diverged over whether poetry should be intellectual or imaginative, personal or political, traditional, new or popular, or whether value was merely a matter of individual taste. In anthologies produced in the 1930s, the editors' selections were justified by introducing new writers, by choosing poems which were representative of current trends or previously unpublished pieces, by their relation to ordinary speech or by being 'good' (undefined). In other words, there was no consensus about a good poem nor a uniformity of practice from which women could collectively be dismissed. The poets did not constitute a single social group with shared characteristics or experiences. The diversity of poetry by women discounts simplistic generalisations about women's poetry and yet it seems as if these poets were themselves discounted, albeit unconsciously and unintentionally, for being women.

Women and poetry in the 1930s

Women were especially conscious of change in their own histories; the new freedoms aroused mixed feelings and created differences between women. During the First World War a hundred thousand had become nurses and half a million had worked in munitions factories. They had taken over men's work and, temporarily, men's rates of pay. In 1918, women over 30 were granted the vote and the first woman was elected to parliament.[26] The 1919 Sex Disqualification Act allowed women to be employed by public services. During the 1920s, the universities of Oxford and Cambridge admitted women to degrees, unemployment benefits were extended to include allowances for wives and families, and there were pensions for widows. From 1928 all women over 21 could vote. Gender politics was still active as women fought for the right to combine work with marriage and to work out new roles within the home. In the 1930s, women were particularly concerned with the differences between the married and the single woman; women who had gained an autonomy and significance in the war resented having to give up their careers for marriage and motherhood. In a broadcast talk, 'Can Men and Women be Really Equal?', Ellen Wilkinson, MP, argued that new employment opportunities could only be enjoyed by single women: 'Today there is an ever-increasing number of married women who are wondering whether they really are pulling their weight in the world's work; whether the talk of the modern equality does not in fact, cover up dependence and not a little futility.'[27] Winifred Holtby, however, represented single women who had either been brought up without a profession or who had trained but been unable to find employment: in both cases they remained dependent upon their families:

> [I am] an unmarried woman of thirty four whose parents live in a small provincial town ... I am an ex-guide patrol leader; I have done that nursing and training mentioned by Mrs Case; I have, I believe, the usual domestic accomplishments of plain sewing and invalid cookery. I have been a school manager, taught in Sunday School and have been secretary of several voluntary associations. It is out of intimate personal experience that I write, when I say that I have never yet met an unmarried woman of over thirty who leads from free choice the life of a 'daughter at home' as the most desirable vocation in the world. Either she is waiting in hopes of marriage, or she has abandoned hope and is resigned. As the life-work of a civilised adult, I find resignation inadequate.[28]

Although the position of women was still restricted, the financially independent had unprecedented opportunities for employment, freer speech and travel. They ran publishing houses, bookshops and journals and they became editors, reviewers and journalists. Laura Riding (with Robert Graves) ran the Seizin Press and a critical periodical. Nancy Cunard started the Hours Press; Dorothy Wellesley edited the Hogarth Living Poets series; Anne Ridler worked with T.S. Eliot at Faber & Faber. Winifred Holtby was a director of *Time and Tide* and E.J. Scovell was among its editors. Sylvia Townsend Warner became an executive committee member for the Association of Writers for Intellectual Liberty; she and Valentine Ackland belonged to the Left Book

Club and went as aid workers to the Spanish Civil War. Nancy Cunard also took up the cause of the Spanish Republicans and published the ground-breaking anthology *Negro* (1934). Janet Adam Smith was instrumental in the poetry programmes on the radio and edited the anthology of broadcast poems, *Poems of Tomorrow*, in 1935. During the war, and later, when her husband's ill-health prevented him from doing so, Alida Monro ran The Poetry Bookshop, which was a meeting point for poets as well as a marketing and publishing industry.[29] All twenty poets published collections of their own and several other women were evidently successful in seeing individual poems in print.

These achievements are all the more remarkable when the poets were mostly working in isolation and when getting published was not easy for women. In spite of gaining certain rights, discouragement and limitation are suggested through the use of pseudonyms, from the posthumous reputations of Stevie Smith and Sylvia Townsend Warner and through Anna Wickham's story of being sent to an asylum when her husband learned that her poems had been accepted for publication.[30] As women, it was difficult to penetrate literary circles; they lacked the publicity and promotion which are achieved through making the right social connections; they could not easily integrate into their respective socio-literary milieus as they were often pressed by social duties, cultural constraints and family responsibilities. Unlike her son John, for example, Frances Cornford could not exchange views and compositions with the young men at the Arts Cafe in Parton Street. Although acquainted with writers from the Woolfs to Walter de la Mare, she was prevented from closer intimacy by family ties in Cambridge. Edith Sitwell left home and braved the London scene; her tea parties and soirées for literary colleagues were well supported, but gave her a reputation for eccentricity, partly, no doubt, on account of being a woman on her own. As a single woman looking after an ailing aunt, Stevie Smith was limited in her ability to engage socially with London poets. As a woman, she felt an outsider in the literary world.[31] Laura Riding, also something of a public figure, was, like Edith Sitwell and Stevie Smith, considered an oddity and more attention was given to her liaison with Robert Graves than to her work. Her sense of artistic isolation was presumably shared by many women:

Where are those other-than-male-voices ...? I am aware of no
explicit others; I say this without any personalistic pleasure in
being 'alone'. But one woman goes a long way – in any capacity.[32]

Laura Riding was not alone, but geographical distances and lack
of constructive publicity made it seem so, especially for an
American 'outsider'. Sylvia Townsend Warner attributes the
overlooking of early women writers to the fact that they 'only
went off one at a time' and not collectively.[33] There were,
nevertheless, some associations between the women: Vita
Sackville-West, Dorothy Wellesley, Edith Sitwell and Lilian
Bowes Lyon were all from aristocratic stock and attended some
of the same social occasions in London. Sylvia Townsend Warner,
Valentine Ackland, Nancy Cunard, Naomi Mitchison and Stevie
Smith were united by their left-wing commitment and activities;
Anna Wickham and Nancy Cunard, were, in varying degrees,
part of the artistic circle for women in Paris, associated with such
figures as Gertrude Stein, Djuna Barnes and Natalie Barney.
Some long lasting relationships developed between some of the
women and some corresponded. Any intimacies or encounters,
however, tended to be personal rather than professional: they
rarely exchanged or discussed their poems.

Several women were, and have continued to be, overshadowed
by the more public profiles of their counterparts: Frances Cornford was usually linked to her grandfather, sons or to her
husband; Edith Sitwell to her brothers; Elizabeth Daryush to her
father, Robert Bridges, and Vita Sackville-West to Virginia
Woolf. Although Laura Riding's verdict was that Robert Graves'
devotion to herself exceeded hers to him, she continues to be a
victim of scandal in literary discourses. The complexities of
circumstances do not, however, permit a simple solution of
conspiratorial male rejection, both at the time or since. It is
understandable that, as in the 1920s, women welcomed the
necessary promotion of literary men. W.B. Yeats and Dorothy
Wellesley were mutual admirers and T.S. Eliot encouraged Anne
Ridler to 'go on' with her writing. David Garnett supported Anna
Wickham, Vita Sackville-West and Sylvia Townsend Warner in
their attempts to get published. These individual men, however,
encouraged *publication*. Critical *reception* was not so generous.

Even though women's publications were usually acknowledged in the poetry papers, reviewers were reluctant to identify their achievements and gave little attention to the poetry. Kathleen Raine, the most successful woman at getting her poems into journals and poetry papers, was championed by Geoffrey Grigson, but not by the Cambridge poets. She records the inhibiting atmosphere of schoolboy rivalry with its point-scoring and one-upmanship:

> I assumed that those who claimed to be poets and who acclaimed one another, must know (since they looked upon me as a naive creature) not less but more about poetry than I. When I met these writers of my generation, some of whom have since become famous, I assumed that when they made pronouncements upon poetry that they and I were discussing the same thing. I did not like their poems any more than they liked mine (and they were more right than I), even though they would have disliked my work still more had it been better ... I attributed it to my ignorance and kept very quiet.[34]

I have met the three other poets who are still alive to tell of how difficult it was to be a 'poet' and not a 'woman'. E.J. Scovell remembers being conscious of a prevailing taste for the Auden-esque which stopped her from trying to get published; according to Anne Ridler,

> It was difficult for women poets to achieve publication in the 1930s and still more difficult to be treated as a poet pure and simple, rather than as a woman poet.[35]

and according to Naomi Mitchison,

> Looking back to the Thirties, there was Auden and co. and they wouldn't accept females as verse writers, at least that is how I remember them (not so much Auden himself, but his followers, few of whom were that good). Everything is made more difficult for women.[36]

In the changing cultural climate, the perception of the woman as poet was obviously a problem for all these writers. The forceful objection to being a 'woman poet' reflects its derogatory status at the beginning of the century. Kathleen Raine refuses to be involved in discussions on gender and Frances Cornford put down her own lack of sympathy with anthologies of women's verse to 'the horror in which all right-thinking people must hold the word "Poetess". She, we all feel, is somebody with far too much fervent personal emotion'.[37] Edith Sitwell's denouncement of her sex seems surprising, but it was probably merely a wish to be disassociated from a line of writing perceived as weak and valueless:

> Women's poetry ... except Sappho, 'Goblin Market' and a few deep and concentrated but fearfully incomplete poems of Emily Dickinson is simply awful ... incompetent, floppy, whining, arch, trivial, self-pitying.[38]

Stevie Smith's later poem 'Miss Snooks' parodies the expectation of a woman poet to be 'awfully nice' and Anna Wickham's 'Explanation' confronts the prejudices against the woman artist.[39] In 1925, Sylvia Townsend Warner had written, 'But as I am only woman ... /With piteous human care /I have made this poem ... /And set it on the shelf with the rest to be.'[40]

The degree of respect for women poets was largely determined by the poet critics. Male reviewers did not know how to assess poetry by women, so they left it alone, dismissed it or wrote about it obliquely. These women consciously resisted anything which might align them to the perceived tradition of sentimentalised verse; because they did not conform to the poetess image, reviewers did not know where to place them. There was undoubted resistance to women's infiltration into the venerated sphere of literary activity. One editor, for example, was more interested in T.S. Eliot's introduction to Marianne Moore's *Selected Poems* than its content;[41] Edith Sitwell wondered why her appearance had become a 'national problem';[42] a reviewer of Laura Riding's *The Life of the Dead* advised her to try yoga;[43] Ruth Pitter's prizewinning poetry was denounced as 'fake'.[44] Geoffrey Grigson's sneering counter-attacks on Edith Sitwell are notorious. These condemnations were not, of course, widely held judgements – the circulation of *New Verse* was about one thousand – nor were they aimed exclusively at women. It does, however, seem that it is the myths about women collectively which worked against the individual, for there are no convincing proofs of inferiority. Furthermore, wherever the poetry has been rediscovered, it has been pronounced 'neglected' rather than 'bad': '[Ruth Pitter] ... unwarrantably neglected'[45]; '[the poems of Sylvia Townsend Warner] ... the greatest inattention of the literary world'[46]; '[E.J. Scovell] ... probably the best neglected poet in the country'[47]; '[Anna Wickham's neglect] ... one of the great mysteries of contemporary literature'[48]; 'Elizabeth Daryush ... suffered from neglect on the part of the British public, her work being better known in America.'[49]

The poems

I have selected poems which articulate and represent the sense of change in the period, which extend the orthodox categories of Thirties poetry by connecting to recognisable themes – war, social justice, modernity – or which introduce specifically female experience, especially conflicting attitudes towards family duty or to being single; across these strands I have tried to represent the range of each poet's work at the time.

Most poets wrote about wars. Warner's, Ackland's and Cunard's poems on Spain were written from firsthand experience whereas others like 'Battlefield' by Lilian Bowes Lyon or Kathleen Raine's 'Fata Morgana', composed in 1936, were second-hand responses to the Spanish Civil War. The poems entitled '1939' by Vita Sackville-West and Dorothy Wellesley express the universal despair which superseded party politics at the end of the decade. Anne Ridler wrote several poems at the onset of the Second World War and Naomi Mitchison's 'Thinking of War' is typical of many poems which use images from the First World War to express the sense of never-ending war which became increasingly prevalent after 1936.

Some poems are overtly party political like Valentine Ackland's 'Communist Poem 1935' or Naomi Mitchison's 'To Some Young Communists from an Older Socialist'. The politics or social conscience in many poems is less explicit in that they question experience or received wisdom. For example, Sylvia Townsend Warner is forcibly ironic and Ruth Pitter gently satiric in their treatment of institutionalised oppression and Stevie Smith characteristically undermines the complacency of traditionalism and the inhumanity of bureaucracy. Poems, such as 'Invalid

Dawn', by Elizabeth Daryush or 'The Man Who Hated the Spring' by Winifred Holtby, dwell on the mixed blessings of industrialisation and technological progress. Stevie Smith interrogates the relationship between high and low cultures in 'Portrait' or 'Salon d'Automne'; the audacity of her apparent irreverence for received pronunciation and elitist art is difficult to gauge from the perspective of the 1990s where such postmodern strategies are now commonplace.

In many of these poems, the gender of composition seems indeterminable. Whether indeterminacy of gender in a woman's writing is to be applauded or lamented is the durable hinge of the feminist debate which swings on the possibility of creating an identifiable woman's language; it asks whether women writing as men are hampered by the inherited paradigms of patriarchy. Laura Riding said that women were ineffectual when they 'assume the rehearsal-manner of men'[50] and Edith Sitwell advised women to 'forge their own technique'.[51] These two poets' own practices, however, are often not easily distinguishable as feminine. To illustrate both the manliness and the womanliness of women's poems is not to have and eat a woman-only cake, but to recognise their breadth of vision and their stylistic ranges. It is also crucial to recognise that in their cultural contexts they would have been writing as men in order to get published and to avoid the 'poetess' stigma. It is appropriate and rewarding to recognise the technical virtuosity of the poets in the wider context of British poetry; the innovative experiments of Edith Sitwell or Elizabeth Daryush, for instance, have to be assessed within the traditions that they knew.

At the same time, there are features which indicate a definable female aesthetic in terms of perspective and subject matter. Women inevitably wrote more about women. Even where the experience which informs the poem is universal, the woman poet often chooses a woman as her subject. The gap between desire and fulfilment, for example, is sometimes presented as a human one, and at other times as specific to the female sex. The most obvious gender specific subject matter is the physiological experience of womanhood and sexual identity. Anne Ridler's 'The Crab is In' is a rare poem on menstruation. There are many poems of motherhood, courtship and marriage which present a variety of moods although there is little celebration. Instead, the burden of duty and the attractions of individual liberty echo through the poems. The prevailing sentiments are the frustration of having responsibility without privilege, and coerced gratitude. Women in the 1930s were under some obligation to be thankful for their new equality of status; the married and financially comfortable woman was counted as being particularly lucky, but the growing centrality of the home brought pressures to find satisfaction within the family circle: secure but stultifying. Where there is optimism in these poems, it is often a constructed cheeriness which barely clothes the despairing mind. In 'Maternal Love Triumphant' by Ruth Pitter, the supposed joys of mother-hood are treated with heavy irony although the ending attempts to reinforce them. The fear of not-waving-but-drowning is the essence of 'Boats in the Bay', by Winifred Holtby, and Frances Cornford's 'Ode on the Whole Duty of Parents', skilfully pays lip-service to conventional joys whilst uncovering the disquietude beneath the performed roles expected of women. Frances Cornford's journals, like Anna Wickham's *Fragment of an Autobiography*, disclose the underwater tugs, described by Alison Light as 'the unquiet depths beneath the apparently unruffled surface of women living between the wars'.[52]

The poems in *Time and Tide* further record the mixture of acquiescence and resistance of women to their lot. These verses, however, are unrefined and operate as outlets for the competing impulses of self-denial and self-realisation. The clichés and mo-notonous rhythms record a superficial adherence to received codes of identity and self-expression; they distinguish the latent from the active feminist and the under-developed from the professional poet. The more adventurous and accomplished poets succeed in fictionalising the subject; they are also good at telling stories. E.J. Scovell, Anna Wickham and Stevie Smith, respec-tively, evoke life in a glimpsed moment in 'The Poor Mother', 'The Sick Assailant' and 'Marriage I Think'. Tales of seduction and disappointment are abundant and betrayal is presented as common to all social rungs. In some of Anna Wickham's portraits, both men and women are prey to culturally prescribed expecta-tions of masculinity and femininity.

Although the marketing of Hollywood films and romantic

fiction was a commercial success with the upsurge in cinemas, popular women's weeklies and Mills & Boon novels, nowhere is romantic love glamorised in these poems. In 'Beauty, the Lover's Gift,' Winifred Holtby objects to the demands on women to be both mantelpiece objects and servants. The rewriting of myths which represent women as paragons of altruism or moral rectitude is a device which connects to women's writing across cultural boundaries and genres; it is a way of rejecting men's versions of women's natures, and of reshaping the world as women see it. Anna Wickham frequently inverts sentimentalised chivalric and pastoral ideals and in 'Tess', Vita Sackville-West deconstructs Thomas Hardy's portrayal of the heroic. The tongues of other silenced heroines are unlocked in 'Song of Ophelia the Survivor' by Anna Wickham and 'Fanny Brawne's Letter Put Unopened in Keats's Coffin' by Valentine Ackland. Reversal of stereotype is now a more hackneyed, but nevertheless an effective, political strategy and encouraged by Sandra Gilbert and Susan Gubar;[53] Naomi Mitchison, for example, enjoys presenting the woman as emotionally, if not actively, footloose.

Poems about shared love are remarkably few and difficult to categorise. There is nothing of the confessional, even if there is conversational intimacy. The love songs of Valentine Ackland and Sylvia Townsend Warner, such as in the title poem of *Whether a Dove or a Seagull* are the most lyrical. These, like some by Vita Sackville-West, should be read in the light of a lesbian aesthetic of mutuality and coded declaration.

Most striking is the number of poems about women alone. Isolation may be considered as a recurring motif in women's writing generally, but singleness was a particularly real position or prospect for women who had either been bereaved of spouse or who were bereft of likely male partners after the First World War. The solitary females portrayed, however, are not necessarily pitiable: they often appear to cherish their independence as much as they regret the accompanying loneliness. The treatment of the single life is ambivalent – there is a celebration of independence mixed with frustration caused by the social restriction on women on their own. Sylvia Townsend Warner records being 'absorbed by the fascinating discipline of living alone' when she first earned a salary and supported herself in London.[54] 'The Single Woman'

(Frances Cornford), 'Spinster' (Vita Sackville-West), 'The Solitary' (Sylvia Lynd) and 'The Blind Tramp' (Lilian Bowes Lyon) are unsettling portrayals of the unattached; solitude is hauntingly depicted in E.J. Scovell's 'Suicide', but 'The Lonely Woman' (Valentine Ackland), Ruth Pitter's, 'Old, Childless, Husbandless' or Vita Sackville-West's 'The Dream' suggest the strength and possibilities in self-sufficiency and self-containment; the portrayals of a lifetime-in-waiting in 'A Peasant Woman' (Frances Cornford), 'The Woman Knitting' (Lilian Bowes Lyon) and 'Dying of Cancer' (E.J. Scovell) mix admiration with sadness. Only 'Solitude' (Vita Sackville-West) or 'Memories of Mortalities' (Laura Riding) are presented as autobiographies.

In addition to recognising the woman-centredness of much women's poetry, discussions about the identification of a specifically female language, which is culturally and/or biologically determined, seek to circumscribe a distinctive woman's voice.[55] The 'voice', as has been illustrated, is, however, usually fictional and can be multiple or male. These poets refashion experience into constructed monologues and dialogues, or into a story where the narrator is sometimes mocking, gently teasing or enigmatic: when there is simplicity, it is adopted as a mask of naiveté in order to contrast innocence with deceit and thereby to expose hypocrisy and oppression. Anna Wickham and Sylvia Townsend Warner, notably both talented musicians, use the constructed voice with admirable elasticity and effect. Sylvia Townsend Warner herself noted that women are particularly adept at vanishing out of their writing so that the quality of immediacy replaces them: 'the writing is no longer propelled by the author's anxious hand, the reader is no longer conscious of the author's chaperoning presence'.[56] She cites Frances Cornford's poetry as exemplary of this sense that the subjects have not merely been described but have been reconstructed. The speaker, then, is rarely the author and never didactic. More fruitful, therefore, than defining a 'woman's voice' in the poems is identifying a woman's consciousness or way of seeing. Sylvia Townsend Warner put it down to a difference of circumstance and explained how women were able to find 'an ease in low company' and could look out of the 'pantry window', which means that, 'viewing life through that window, they have achieved what those running the castle have missed.'[57] The most frequent challenges to those running the home or the country made by these women is in their portrayal of the effects of legislation, institutions, wars, particular men or change on the individual.

Question marks are common and another means of challenge. This questioning sometimes represents powerlessness but it is often rhetorical. Dorothy Wellesley's or Elizabeth Daryush's voices of dissatisfaction and irony are not necessarily apologetic or reticent, but, as Jem Poster observed of E.J. Scovell, they can set up alternative ways of seeing: 'The very act of questioning can itself be regarded as a gesture of enlargement, a means of exerting pressure against the boundaries of experience.'[58]

In this discussion, I may have appeared to separate the poems into the political and the woman-centred, but I have also tried to demonstrate how gender intersects with politics and writing and that labelling can be misleading: a simplistic differentiation between 'woman's' or 'political' issues can risk excluding poems and writers that do not fit and it is the difficulty of classifying poetry which has often led to its dismissal. Sylvia Townsend Warner, for instance, has slipped between categories:

> an exile from the pages of literary history ... her politics labelled radical in the social text of the twentieth century and her poetic and fictional forms conservative in the Modernist canonical text, she is known by the epithet – *lady* communist, as Stephen Spender sarcastically dismissed her, and a *communist* writer who contributed to the *Left Review* as those who purport to write the literary histories of the Spanish Civil War and the 1930s list her.[59]

Paradoxically, Sylvia Townsend Warner's combination of the conservative and the modern is, in fact, a discernible aesthetic of the period, but for being awkwardly individual, radical yet traditional, and, of course, female, she has lain in a no man's land.

Women have been exiled from and need to be replaced into literary history. If this were not the case, the feminist commitment to challenge grouping and to deconstruct historicism should question a separatist and period-bound text such as this, particularly since two of the poets, Kathleen Raine and Laura Riding, refused to be part of a women's anthology and that several others clearly wished to be disengaged from demarcation by gender.

The politics of the collection, however, is that in combination, the poets defy a global theory of either women's or Thirties poetry and although I am conscious of the tendency of editors of gender specific anthologies to announce the diversity of the poetry selected, it remains true that what is remarkable about the poetry here is the range.

The range of poets means that it is advisable to give them all an attentive eye and, in particular, an attentive ear. If consensus over a 'good poem' is neither desirable nor possible, value is largely determined by context. These poems can be read in terms of a tradition of women's poetry and also read in terms of the decade and for the ways in which they represent the mixed poetic visions and styles of the period. Anna Wickham commands attention to sexual politics whereas Valentine Ackland explores same-sex love. Sylvia Townsend Warner can be outstanding for her poetic journalism and Anne Ridler's poems on the incipient World War are the most effective for their representation of the responses to the News; Stevie Smith's portraits are memorable depictions of social injustice and of the paradoxical relationship between individualism and isolation which characterised much of the art of the 1930s. The portraits by E.J. Scovell and Frances Cornford stand out for their combinations of observation and evocation.

In order to resist the tendency towards hierarchical evaluation, however, I would encourage preferences between poems rather than poets. It is also genuinely difficult to compare, say, Vita Sackville-West in 1934 to Dorothy Wellesley in 1939 or Sylvia Townsend Warner in 1936. Making connections with well analysed poets is always tempting and can be illuminating, but can also be fatuous. Sylvia Townsend Warner, for example, has been variously linked with the Metaphysicals, Thomas Hardy and T.E. Powys; she could equally merit the accolade which Herbert Read afforded to Auden: '[he] brought a new vitality into English verse, an exuberance which it has lacked since Browning's death. His idiom is contemporary, his outlook is revolutionary. He is human and observant, witty and masculine.'[60] The new vitality was not, and never has been, exclusively masculine, but it is the 'new vitality' to which the late twentieth-century readers will respond most readily – poetry which has a conversational idiom and psychological interest – because this is what we are used to in modern and contemporary poetry; hence, it is likely that there will be preferences for poems by Anna Wickham, Stevie Smith, Nancy Cunard, Naomi Mitchison, Sylvia Townsend Warner and Frances Cornford. Vita Sackville-West's 'Sissinghurst' or Sylvia Lynd's poems may have vestiges of so-called Georgian poeticism but that in itself does not make them bad poetry; the style was still popular at the beginning of the decade and the outlook of the poets is not old-fashioned; traditional is not synonymous with traditionalist.

To sum up: I have tried to illustrate that through their interrogations of national and international affairs, their preoccupations with cultural politics and their experiments with language and form, these women exert pressure on our understanding of poetry in the 1930s and that collectively their poems strengthen the feminist project which rejects the language of centrality and dominance in favour of diversity and difference.

Notes

1 Virginia Woolf, 'The Leaning Tower', *A Woman's Essays*, Harmondsworth, Penguin, 1992, pp. 159–78.

2 Ellen Wilkinson MP, 'Can Men and Women be Really Equal?' *The Listener*, 2 April 1930, pp. 587–8. Ellen Wilkinson was a Labour MP admired by Winifred Holtby. See Vera Brittain, *Testament of Friendship*, London, Virago, 1980, p. 420.

3 David Dean, *The Thirties: Recalling the English Architectural Scene*, London, Trefoil Books Ltd, 1983, p. 8.

4 T.S. Eliot, *The Little Book of Modern Verse*, ed. Anne Ridler, London, Faber, 1941, p. 7.

5 See, for example, Adrian Caesar, *Dividing Lines: Poetry, Class and Ideology in the 1930s*, Manchester, Manchester University Press, 1991.

6 Allan Rodway's *Poets of the 1930s*, London, Longman, 1967, has no women; Robin Skelton's *Poetry of the Thirties*, Harmondsworth, Penguin, 1964, reprinted several times, contains three poems by Anne Ridler.

7 Jack Barbera and William McBrien, eds, *Me Again: The Uncollected Writings of Stevie Smith*, London, Virago, 1981.

8 H.M. Shire, ed., *The Pure Account: Poems of Olive Fraser*, Aberdeen University Press, 1981; *The Wrong Music: The Poems of Olive Fraser*, Edinburgh, Canongate, 1989.

9 Professor Bronislaw, 'The Present Crisis of Marriage No 1', *The Listener*, 7 January 1931, pp. 7–8.

10 Donald Davie, ed., *Elizabeth Daryush: Collected Poems*, Manchester, Carcanet, 1976, p. 13.

11 Jeni Couzyn, ed., *The Bloodaxe Book of Contemporary Women Poets*, Newcastle upon Tyne, Bloodaxe Books, 1985, p. 14.

12 G. Grigson, ed., *Poetry of the Present: An Anthology of the Thirties and After*, London, Phoenix House, 1949, p. 24.

13 W.B. Yeats, *The Listener*, 14 October 1936, p. 697.

14 Cyril Connolly, 'Comment', *Horizon*, no. 2, February 1940, pp. 68–71.

15 Stephen Spender, *The Thirties and After: Poetry, Politics, People 1933–75*, London, Collins/Fontana, 1978, p. 9.

16 T.S. Eliot, *The Little Book of Modern Verse*, p. 7.

17 Robin Skelton, *Poetry of the Thirties*, p. 30.

18 Virginia Woolf, 'The Leaning Tower', p. 169.

19 MacSpaunday was the name given by the poet Roy Campbell to Louis MacNeice, Stephen Spender, W.H. Auden and C. Day Lewis. See R. Carter, ed., *Thirties Poets: 'The Auden Group'*, London, Macmillan, 1984, p. 12.

20 The Mass Observation Movement was instigated by the sociologist Tom Harrisson, the critic Humphrey Jennings and the poet Charles Madge in 1937. It aimed to document the ordinary lives of ordinary people, especially northerners, ostensibly for 'the scientific control of society', but also for their artistic possibilities. See Julian Symons, ch. 11, 'Mass Observation', *The Thirties: A Dream Revolved*, (London, The Cresset Press, 1960), London, Faber, 1975, pp. 101–5.

21 Virginia Woolf, 'The Leaning Tower', p. 169.

22 ibid., p. 168.

23 ibid., p. 173.

24 ibid.

25 'Into the Whirlwind', is from Anne Ridler, *Some Time After and Other Poems*, London, Faber, 1972.

26 Countess Marckiewicz was elected to Parliament in 1918; Nancy Astor was the first woman MP to actually take her seat in 1919.

27 Ellen Wilkinson MP, 'Can Men and Women be Really Equal?', *The Listener*, p. 587.

28 'Tea-Table Sitters', letter from Winifred Holtby to *Time and Tide*, 31 December 1932, p. 1437. She is responding to a letter by Mrs Cardew and Mrs Case.

29 See letters from Edith Sitwell and Alida Monro, *Time and Tide*, 2 April and 9 April 1932, pp. 371, 395, respectively.

30 See David Garnett's Introduction to *Selected Poems by Anna Wickham*, London, Chatto & Windus, 1971.

31 Stevie Smith, letter to Naomi Mitchison in Frances Spalding, *Stevie Smith: A Critical Biography*, London, Faber, 1988, p. 126.

32 Laura Riding, 'An Enquiry', *New Verse*, no. 11, October 1934, p. 5.

33 Sylvia Townsend Warner, 'Women as Writers', Lecture to the Royal Society of Arts, 11 February 1959, published in the journal of the RSA, May 1959, pp. 378–86; see Appendix, *CP*, Manchester, Carcanet, 1982, p. 265.

34 Kathleen Raine, 'On the Symbol', *Defending Ancient Springs*, Oxford, Oxford University Press, 1967, p. 104.

35 Anne Ridler, letter to Jane Dowson, 1 September 1992.

36 Naomi Mitchison, letter to Jane Dowson, undated, 1993.

37 Frances Cornford, 'Views and Recollections of a Sunday Poet', 27 March 1956, *The Literary Papers of Frances Cornford*, Add. Mss. 58387, Department of Manuscripts, London, British Library.

38 'Selected Letters', Elizabeth Salter and Allanah Harper, eds, *Edith Sitwell: Fire of the Mind. An Anthology*, London, Michael Joseph (1956) 1976, p. 188.

39 For 'Explanation', see section on Anna Wickham.

40 Sylvia Townsend Warner, 'Wish in Spring', *Selected Poems*, Manchester, Carcanet, 1985, p. 68.

41 Geoffrey Grigson, review of *SP*, Marianne Moore, *New Verse*, no. 15, June 1935, p. 21.

42 Edith Sitwell, 'Self-Portrait', in Elizabeth Salter and Allanah Harper, eds, *Edith Sitwell: Fire of the Mind*, p. 105.

43 Louis MacNeice, Review of Laura Riding, *The Life of the Dead*, *New Verse*, no. 6, December 1933, p. 19.

44 Stephen Spender, 'Christmas Books', *New Statesman and Nation*, 9 December 1939, p. 834.

45 Peter Dickinson, *Independent*, 2 March 1992, p. 14.

46 Claire Harman, *PN Review*, 23, vol. 8, no. 3, 1981, p. 30.

47 Editor's Comment, 'A Visionary in Sensible Shoes', *Poetry Review*, vol. 76, no. 4, December 1986, p. 37.

48 R.D. Smith, ed., *The Writings of Anna Wickham: Free Woman and Poet*, London, Virago, 1984, back cover.

49 'Tribute', *The Times*, 9 April 1977, p. 14.

50 Laura Riding, 'An Enquiry', *New Verse*, October 1934, no. 11, p. 5.

51 Edith Sitwell, in Elizabeth Salter and Allanah Harper, eds, *Edith Sitwell: Fire of the Mind*, p. 188.

52 Alison Light, *Forever England: Femininity, Literature and Conservatism Between the Wars*, London, Routledge, 1994, p. 13.

53 S. Gilbert and S. Gubar, 'Gender, Creativity and the Woman Poet', *Shakespeare's Sisters: Feminist Essays on Women Poets*, Bloomington, Indiana University Press, 1979, p. xv.

54 Sylvia Townsend Warner, 'The Way By Which I Have Come', *Countryman*, xix, no. 2, 1939, p. 476.

55 See, for example, Deborah Cameron, *Feminism and Linguistic Theory*, Macmillan, Basingstoke, 1992.

56 Sylvia Townsend Warner, 'Women as Writers', *CP*, p. 269.

57 Barbara Brothers, citing Sylvia Townsend Warner, 'Women as Writers'. See 'Writing Against the Grain: Sylvia Townsend Warner and the Spanish Civil War', in *Women's Writing in Exile*, eds. Mary Lynn Broe and Angela Ingram, 1989, Chapel Hill, University of North Carolina Press, 1989, p. 352.

58 Jem Poster, 'In Love With Space', *PN Review* 90, vol. 19, no. 4, 1988, p. 24.

59 Barbara Brothers, 'Writing Against the Grain: Sylvia Townsend Warner and the Spanish Civil War', p. 362.

60 Herbert Read, 'Sixteen Comments on Auden', *New Verse* 26–7, no. 11, double number on Auden, November 1937, p. 28.

I
Valentine Ackland
1906–1969

1933 *Whether a Dove or a Seagull*, with Sylvia Townsend Warner, New York, Viking; London, Chatto & Windus, 1934

1957 *Twenty Eight Poems*, privately printed, London and Wells, Clare, Son & Co. Ltd

1970 *Later Poems by Valentine Ackland*, London and Wells, Clare, Son & Co. Ltd

1973 *The Nature of the Moment*, London, Chatto & Windus

1978 *Further Poems of Valentine Ackland*, Kent, Welmont Publishing

Mary Kathleen McCrory adopted her androgynous pseudonym 'Valentine Ackland' to rid herself of the nickname 'Molly', when she decided to become a serious poet in the late 1920s. She had an Anglo-Catholic upbringing in Norfolk and a convent school education in London. She was received into the Roman Catholic church when she married in 1925 and she shortly left both her husband and the church. Her marriage was annulled and she returned to her Catholic faith in the 1950s, and finally became a Quaker. She did not, however, in spite of pressure from her family, become reconciled to physical love with a man, even though by 1932 she is alleged to have had twenty-seven affairs, five of which were with men and one of which resulted in a miscarriage in 1927. In 1930, she met Sylvia Townsend Warner with whom she lived, mainly in Dorset, until her own death from cancer. It was Valentine who initiated their involvements with the Communist Party, the Spanish Civil War, and socialist and pacifist activities, but after the Second World War she became more preoccupied with her personal relationships. Valentine's confessional autobiography, *For Sylvia: An Honest Account*, written in 1949, is an attempt to understand, to explain and to exorcise her secret drinking habit of several years and her affair with the American Elizabeth Wade White which had briefly taken her away from Sylvia Townsend Warner. She recounts her recurring and unresolved problem with loving two people simultaneously, but reassures herself that 'I know beyond any doubt that my whole being is rooted in Sylvia'.[1] This combination of conviction and doubt concerning her identity, her Christian faith and her politics is evident in her poetry. She was an avid reader and fervent writer of poetry from childhood; Sylvia Townsend Warner admired in her what she herself found difficult in poetry, 'the lyrical, short and loose formed'.[2] Although Valentine Ackland's poems were published in periodicals throughout the 1930s and 1940s in both America and Britain, she never became what she wanted to be, 'a published, widely read poet'.[3] The collections of her poems have mostly been published posthumously and little has been written about her poetry.

In 1937, Valentine Ackland and Sylvia Townsend Warner moved house from West Chaldon to Frome Vauchurch, near Dorchester, but during the 1930s, they were often away, campaigning for the cause of democracy. The Reichstag Fire Trial in Germany caught their attention in 1933, and although initially suspicious of communists, they subscribed to the *Daily Worker* and *Left Review*, which was set up by Edgell Rickword in 1933, and for which Valentine wrote a series of articles called 'Country Dealings' which exposed the deprived conditions of the rural poor. In 1935, she and Sylvia joined the Communist Party and went to the Congress of Writers in Paris, which was also attended by Winifred Holtby, Storm Jameson and Naomi Mitchison. In 1939 they went to the United States for the 3rd American Writers Congress in New York, to consider the loss of democracy in Europe and returned when war broke out. 'Communist Poem 1935', and 'Winter', which were printed in *Left Review*, register the atmosphere of doom which increased from the middle of the decade onwards.[4] The disillusion of an erstwhile Conservative like Valentine was particularly acute: the sense of everything being rotten in Britain extended to Europe, and by the Second World War was perceived as a universal human condition. These poems also illustrate her difficulties when combining a political polemic with her preferred lyrical mode.

In September 1936, Valentine Ackland and Sylvia Townsend Warner responded to an article by Nancy Cunard, published in the *Daily Worker* and *News Chronicle*, appealing for volunteers to help the Spanish Republicans. They gave assistance to the Red Cross Unit in Barcelona. On returning to England, Valentine Ackland intended to drive a lorry from London to Valencia but was too unwell to go. In 1937, she worked voluntarily at Tythrop House, near Thame, a home for Spanish refugee children. Like Sylvia Townsend Warner, she wrote prose and poetry about her experiences in Spain. *Left Review* not only published her poems, but also her reviews on books about the Spanish War and her translations.[5] 'Instructions from England' is printed in *The Penguin Book of Spanish Civil War Verse*. Its satirical tone indicates her endeavour to find a successful and contemporary aesthetic for a political cause; characteristically, she felt caught between two impulses, the traditional and the new:

> I am still uncertain how to write poetry as it has to be written. Whether to carry
> on ... for the present, trusting that (as has happened before) the difficulty of
> reading a 'new' style will wear off ... Or whether to make a partial return to the

old, simpler forms – renouncing the pleasures of inverting words and phrases; of using three-syllabled words; of using semi-scientific words; of assonance and rhyme ... But we need something really *hard*. Not noisy and bombastic ... but definite and deliberately reasonable, ... well-devised and musical.[6]

Wendy Mulford considers that this professed uncertainty is the mark of Valentine Ackland's poetry and that she is at her best when wrestling with the 'paradox of feeling', as exemplified in the lyrics which represent the 'shifting states of the lovers being'.[7] 'Poem' is one of these and is likely to be a dramatisation of the Warner-Ackland-Wade White triangle. The other love poems here are taken from *Whether a Dove or a Seagull*, the co-operative volume which was an experiment in democracy by not divulging the authorship of individual poems. It was also an attempt by Sylvia Townsend Warner to help Valentine Ackland get her poems published. The poems' exploration of lesbian sexuality in a society where it was forbidden may account for the book's poor sales. Valentine Ackland's poems depict the poet's characteristic dualities in their mixture of celebration and frustration. The title poem typically juxtaposes the voice which sings of love with the commentary of realism which insists on the instability of relationship. In 'Overnight' and 'What must we do, if we cannot do this –' the combined agony and ecstasy of secrecy provide the nervous energy of the rhythms. 'The eyes of body' is the most overtly erotic poem in the collection.

It is tempting, and in Valentine Ackland's case, also appropriate, to read the poems in terms of the poet's personality: always in two minds of optimism and dread. The voice of the poems is simultaneously self-negating and self-asserting. As lover, she both wishes for and fears emotional dependency. 'The Lonely Woman' at first seems to endorse the stereotype of the unhappy spinster or widow, but there is also subtle affirmation of the woman's independence and of the quietude which can belong to the unattached. The story of Fanny Brawne's unopened letter is brief and tragic, but again there is some suggestion of private exaltation amidst her solitude and secrecy.

The editor of *Further Poems* detects a consistent exploration of technique in the uncollected poems which span 40 years, and a new dimension to the poems of terminal illness. After Valentine Ackland's death, Sylvia Townsend Warner began work on a collected edition of the poems but found her own grief too overwhelming to be able to write an introduction or to complete the work.

Further Reading

Valentine Ackland, *For Sylvia: An Honest Account*, London, Chatto & Windus, 1985.

Claire Harman, ed., *The Diaries of Sylvia Townsend Warner*, London, Chatto & Windus, 1994.

Wendy Mulford, *This Narrow Place: Sylvia Townsend Warner and Valentine Ackland – Life, Letters and Politics 1930–1951*, London, Pandora, 1988.

Communist Poem, 1935

'What must we do, in a country lost already,
Where already the mills stop, already the factories
Wither inside themselves, kernels smalling in shells,
('Fewer hands – fewer hands') and all the ploughed lands
5   Put down to grass, to bungalows, to graveyards already.

What's in a word? Comrade, while still our country
Seems solid around us, rotting – but still our country.
Comrade is rude, uncouth; bandied among youths
Idle and sick perhaps, wandering with other chaps,
10   Standing around in what is still our country.'

Answer them: Over the low hills and the pastures
Come no more cattle, over the land no more herdsmen;
Nothing against the sky now, no stains show
Of smoke. We're done. Only a few work on,
15   Against time now working to end your time.

Answer: Because the end is coming sooner
Than you allowed for, hail the end as salvation.
Watch how the plough wounds, hear the unlovely sounds
Of sirens wring the air; how everything
20   Labours again, cries out, and again breeds life.

Here is our life, say: Where the dismembered country
Lies, a dead foeman rises a living comrade.
Here where our day begins and your day dims
We part – announce it. And then with lightened heart
Watch life swing round, complete the revolution.

Winter

When the winter closes and the cold and the wet
Come, and there is no morning, no noon-day sun
And no light except half-light until night,
When we lie huddled together, to forget;
5   Then the word moves in us and we stir in our bed,
Clotted together in misery, hungry and time-besotted,
The drag of time on our hands and on nerves the nag,
Then we whisper together and the word we say is red.
Red and angry as the sun will be when it rises,
10   As the furnace-fires we kindle, as the fury which burns us,

The word unspoken in mind, soon to be spoken and heard,
Over screech of sirens when morning comes and the red sun rises.

Left Review, March 1936

Instructions From England
1936

Note nothing of why or how, enquire
no deeper than you need
into what set these veins on fire,
note simply that they bleed.
5   Spain fought before and fights again,
better no question why;
note churches burned and popes in pain
but not the men who die.

Left Review, March 1936

Poem

You send me a letter from far, from across the sea:
'I read of a gale,' you say, 'blowing over your land,
And try to imagine in storm your country
That I saw in sun.' You have stretched out your hand
5   But I cannot take it. A sharper storm had blown
Us apart already, the wind will not slacken but rise
Until we are parted completely –
I overthrown into dust, and you with dust in your eyes.

Time and Tide, 21 August 1937

'Whether a dove or a seagull lighted there'

Whether a dove or a seagull lighted there
I cannot tell,
But on the field that is so green and bare
A whiteness fell –
5   And I must know before I go away
If for today
The weather of our love is wild or fair.
Or ill or well.

'When I have said "I love you"'

When I have said 'I love you' I have said
Nothing at all to tell you; I cannot find
Any speech in any country of the mind
Which might inform you whither I have fled.
5   In saying 'I love you' I have gone so far
Away from you, into so strange a land;
You may not find me, may not understand
How I am exiled, driven to a star

Till now deserted. Here I stand about,
10   Eat, sleep, bewail, feel lonely and explore,
Remember how I loved the world, before,
Tremble in case that memory lets me out.
Islanded here, I wait for you to come –
Waiting the day that exiles you to home.

Overnight

The dark bricks hold the fire alight,
When coals have burned and turned to ash
And grey ashes fallen cold,
Still the dark bricks hold
5   The first fire's heat and flash.

Never lost,
That first tall fire I tossed
Into the grate – too late, I feared,
To warm us as we sat,
10   Strangers, unsure what to be at,
Until the tall fire reared
And we caught,
And burned as quick as thought
When the flames reared and seared, made fire
15   In us, too, bright –
A fire held overnight
In the darkness of our desire.

'What must we do if we cannot do this –'

What must we do if we cannot do this –
Lose ourselves in our dark autumn kiss,
Lose ourselves and each other, and go into the grave,
To rise again in spring, naked and brave?

As cornfields in late summer are
Ripe and dusky, and heavy trees
Weighted with all the summer's care
Stand trembling, so we like these
Must shed our fruit and let the crop
10   Be garnered, and we to winter drop.

Good. Into the dark ground we must go together,
Drawn by our tightened cord, our secret tether;
Here is the grave, the dark grave of our kiss –
We will lie down and be at peace in this.

'The eyes of body'

The eyes of body, being blindfold by night,
Refer to the eyes of mind – at brain's command
Study imagination's map, then order out a hand
To journey forth as deputy for sight.

5   Thus and by these ordered ways
I come at you – Hand deft and delicate
To trace the suavely laid and intricate
Route of your body's maze.

My hand, being deft and delicate, displays
10   Unerring judgement; cleaves between your thighs.
Clean, as a ray-directed airplane flies.

Thus I, within these strictly ordered ways,
Although blindfolded, seize with more than sight
Your moonlit meadows and your shadowed night.

'Blossom, my darling, blossom, be a rose –'

Blossom into a rose as you are bidden,
Woman – Remain at that and be unchidden,
Beloved and love-given, complete –
Or straggle into a tree and have the world at your feet.

[35]

The Lonely Woman

The farm-hands, passing at the end of the day,
Bring the evening paper. Then they go away
And do as they will. I, released from light,
Closed in myself again, do not fear night.
In the wide pages, the flimsy paper, seeing
That others than I are alive and have their being,
And, bright as baubles and gawds in the shops I knew,
Fierce deeds are doing that I never cared to do.

Supper once over, I sit by the fire to read,
And the womb of my heart is barrened and ceases to breed
And I am at peace, who all the day have gone
Teased by its fancies and angry at being alone.
But now I am happy, and read, and do not think
For an hour or more, till I fold the sheet and blink,
And rise to light my candle and climb to bed –
Beneath the low lintel stooping my tired head.

Fanny Brawne's Letter
Put Unopened In Keats's Coffin

'Often, before I came to lie down here, I wept,
And over you – who lie here, silent and diminished,
The seal unbroken. Desire and sorrow long ago were finished –
Long ago now I came, lay down by you, and slept.'

Notes

1 Valentine Ackland, *For Sylvia*, p. 132.
2 Claire Harman, *Sylvia Townsend Warner: A Biography*, London, Chatto & Windus, 1985, p. 112.
3 ibid.
4 'Communist Poem 1935', *Left Review*, vol. 1, no. 10, July 1935, p. 430. 'Winter', *Left Review*, vol. 2, no. 6, March 1936, p. 250.
5 Valentine Ackland's translation of Louis Aragon's 'Waltz', *Left Review*, vol. 1, no. 1, October 1934, pp. 3–5.
6 Letter to Julius Lipton, 1935; Wendy Mulford, *This Narrow Place*, p. 207.
7 Wendy Mulford, *This Narrow Place*, p. 208.

2
Frances Bellerby
1889–1975

1946 *Plash Mill and Other Poems*, London, Peter Davies
1949 *The Brightening Cloud and Other Poems*, London, Peter Davies
1957 *The Stone Angel and the Stone Man*, Plymouth, Ted Wilkins
1970 *The Stuttering Water*, Kent, ARC 7
1970 *Selected Poems*, ed. Charles Causley, London, Enitharmon
1972 *A Possible Prayer for New Year's Day*, one poem, privately printed
1975 *The First-Known and Other Poems*, London, Enitharmon
1975 *In Memory of Frances Bellerby*, (two poems and photograph), London, Enitharmon
1986 *Selected Poems*, ed. Anne Stevenson, introduced by Robert Gittings, London, Enitharmon

The father of Mary Eirene Frances Parker was an ardent Socialist and Anglican clergyman whose parish was in a deprived area of Bath. The family was poor, but close-knit, and Frances retained her Christian faith until her death from cancer. She was educated at Mortimer House School in Clifton, Bristol, and rejected the restraints associated with femininity – 'prettiness was for girls'.[1] She was exceptionally athletic at school and continued to be active on leaving. In the 1920s she worked as a kennelmaid, taught English, Latin and Games, and worked in the London Office of the *Bristol Times and Mirror*. After she and John Bellerby, a Cambridge economist, married in 1929, they became involved in a voluntary organisation for social welfare which was based on communistic ideals of shared income, as described in Frances' pamphlet *Neighbours* (1931). Six months after her wedding, she had a calamitous fall on the cliffs at Lulworth which left her a semi-invalid for the rest of her life. This was followed by her mother's suicide and her own marital and mental breakdowns. In 1932, she wrote a novel, *Shadowy Bricks*, about a progressive first school, and published a volume of short stories, *Come to an End* in 1939, but counted the Thirties in her 'twelve lost years'[2] until she moved to Cornwall in 1941. It is likely, however, that some of the poems were in embryo, at least, during these years.

Several poems date from 1915, when her brother was killed in action; this bereavement and her own tragic misfortunes no doubt fuelled the vigour of her poems of the Second World War. Charles Causley finds an affinity with her evocation of people and her sense of place, especially in the later poems. Frances Bellerby can be at her best when revising the ballad; this popular form suited her lack of pretentiousness and her political socialism.

Notes

1 Frances Bellerby, Letter to Marjorie Bantock, *SP*, 1986, p. 11.
2 Frances Bellerby, Notebook no. 3, *SP*, 1986, p. 22.

3
Lilian Bowes Lyon
1895–1949

1934 *The White Hare and Other Poems*, London, Cape
1936 *Bright Feather Fading*, London, Cape
1941 *Tomorrow is Revealing*, London, Cape
1943 *Evening in Stepney and Other Poems*, London, Cape
1946 *A Rough Walk Home and Other Poems*, London, Cape
1948 *Collected Poems*, introduced by C. Day-Lewis, London, Cape
1981 *Uncollected Poems*, Edinburgh, Tragara

Lilian Bowes Lyon was born into an aristocratic family as a cousin to the Queen Mother. The contrast between the two distinct worlds which she inhabited – the peaceful countryside in Northumberland and the urban congestion of London – heightened her sense of privilege and led to a life of social action. For several years, she headed the Women's Voluntary Services and in 1942 she moved to a flat in the East End of London, from where she could attend to the wounded. Even when severely injured herself during the Blitz, she continued to provide aid to refugees and children and carried on writing. The poems in *Uncollected Poems*, which were composed after she had lost both legs and the use of both hands, are searing accounts of pain. In 1929, she published a novel, *The Buried Stream*, and during the nineteen thirties her individual poems were printed in several journals, including *Time and Tide* and *The Listener*. They were often anthologised, and her collections of poems were in steady demand.

The early elegies of the Northumbrian countryside do not represent the predominant preoccupations of Bowes Lyon's poetry. C. Day-Lewis detected transitions in her writing: the early phase of *The White Hare* before 1934, rewarding for its 'simplicity'; a middle phase, of over-decoration, as illustrated in the frequently anthologised 'Duchess'; 'the more public preoccupation of her work at the end of the Thirties' and, after 1941, a final phase where she developed a more skilled artistic touch.[1] Whilst acknowledging this evolution, it is important not to overlook the versatility of her work. She experimented equally with the sonnet and less regular structures. Edith Sitwell called her 'a poet of a most rare distinction ... her poems are beautifully shaped'.[2] The audio-visual qualities of a poem like 'Battlefield,' made it particularly popular for radio broadcast.³ Although the diction is often overworked and the vocabulary can be archaic, the combination of rhetorics, one abstract and the other anti-heroic, aligns her with much interwar writing.

Irony was a common device of Thirties poets; the title of 'Pastoral' is ironic. The poem was chosen for *The Year's Poetry* in 1936 and is a response to war, rather than a eulogy of England.⁴ The stereotyped rural scene of ploughed field, village and church is disturbed by images of dead men's bones caught up in mechanisation, while bureaucratic predators hypocritically 'howl' at Harvest Festival. Like 'Battlefield', it conforms to the idea of the poetry of the decade in that it engages with the favoured motif of yesterday, today and tomorrow: the ghost of battle past is summoned to warn of battle future. It also juxtaposes productive agricultural upheaval of the countryside with war's futile ravages of the land. The poet's sensitivity to changing cultural conditions and to the innocent victims of war or of social inequalities are dramatised here and in 'The Blind Tramp' and 'A Refugee.' Day-Lewis attributes Bowes Lyon's acute sensitivity to the blasts of the contemporary world to her own blows of fortune. She draws upon the Northumbrian landscapes of her youth for symbols like 'granite winds grind' and 'oat-field's water-silver sail', with which to depict and interpret her observations. At times, the alliterative compounds seem over-imitative of Gerard Manley Hopkins' but their proliferation in her poetry is shortlived.

Although Lilian Bowes Lyon's inherited wealth allowed her an independence denied to many women, 'A Woman Knitting' suggests an empathy with the solitude and work-weariness of the poem's subject. This poem is an example of the solemn sadness which echoes Christina Rossetti's poetry, but it is less personal. Here, physical and mental pain are interwoven, and the untidy rhythm represents the psychological confusion of a woman who wonders interminably whether or not her life has been well-spent.

Pastoral

> This field has buried men; is browed
> With easy gold; day's Midas touch
> Turns all to richness, only these were ploughed
> By poverty under, pave a roofless church –
> 5   Kindle no saffron cloud.
>
> These nothing want, are nameless loam;
> But hungrier bones we knew as boys
> Stand gauntly erect or swelter out their doom,
> Live grist to the machine that still destroys;
> 10   And wolves sing harvest-home.

On evening lea unearth long sighs,
The lingering testament of their pain;
Tear open this sepulchred acre till they rise
And call Peace hypocrite, who dumbly stain
15   With blood her pastoral skies.

Battlefield

Men in their prime,
Boys venerably young.
With all-unfaded brows, died here upon a time;
So heavy a wrong –
5   How may this black world right who trod them into slime?

Still must our milder suns,
Splintering the stained glass window of a wood,
Be darkly seen through these men's blood
And midnight mutter in her sleep with guns.

A Refugee

Outside your window venerable with light,
The transient dusk, whose tale is never ended,
Paused in a foreigner pausing, used to night
Yet by one lamp vicariously befriended,

5   Learning, as evening learns, that grave allegiance
Only to see through glass and not to share
A kingdom kind, a room's ordained effulgence;
Bound by an honour castaway as air

To bruise no gossamer pane, to break no seal,
10   Briefly as dusk to serve your mellowing altar;
Fate and the night stood steady in his soul,
Who thanked a shadow, fire-defined, for shelter.

The Blind Tramp

Her darkness fell, before her day was done;
But now, profounder light's illiterate cloud,
She needs no eyes; she learns to follow alone
The drifting seed whose random flower is dead.

5   A footsure wanderer wearing the first snow
This woman, like the Year that sometime sinned,
Was never entire with innocence till now;
Her griefs forgiven beneath the seamless ground.

Here swelled the oat-field's water-silver sail
10   Where now the granite winds grind out her fate;
The whitening truth knows neither Spring nor Fall:
Only the mind's vision immaculate.

She loves no landmark now, no singular tree,
And keeps no tryst with memory, none with hope.
15   Some covet life to lose it; some agree
With Christ at last, like dew the sun draws up.

A Woman Knitting

A thousand years the flesh of the wool growing
Between my fingers, cast on or cast off
by shifting needles, by the unfertile bone,
The sturdily-flowing
5   wool was, for a thousand years, the tough
smooth strand of life, and I, the woman vigilant,
   wore my heavy crown.

The future between finger and thumb, informed,
fulfilled, made ponderable by the weight of longing, how must I
   wear it,
now my vision mended
10   is strictly wound into a ball of pain?
Whence came the wild-bee stitches warmly thronging
as though mid-summer's murmuring thoughts had swarmed?
Ah bloom of flesh! A thousand years are ended,
and I, the spirit, the vagrant, am uncrowned again.

Notes

1 See C. Day Lewis, Introduction to *CP*, 1948.
2 Edith Sitwell, 'The Poetry of Miss Bowes Lyon', *New Statesman and Nation*, 9 October, 1948, p. 306
3 'Battlefield' was printed in the *The Listener*, 27 February, 1935, p. 380
4 'Pastoral' was printed in the *London Mercury*, March 1932, and in *Best Poetry*, 1932.

4
Frances Cornford
1886–1960

Frances Cornford has been overshadowed by the reputations of her grandfather Charles Darwin (1809–1882), her husband Francis, who was a philosopher and classical scholar, and two of her five talented children: the artist, Christopher, and the oldest son John, who, at the age of 21, was killed fighting for the Spanish Republicans in 1936. Frances' mother Ellen, née Wordsworth Crofts, was a fellow and lecturer in English Literature at Newnham College, Cambridge. After her mother's death in 1903, Frances and her father nearly moved to London, but the decision to stay in Cambridge meant that they remained on the edges of literary circles. Nevertheless, she had a successful publishing record while she was alive. Her first books were quickly out of print and reprinted within a year. Her inclusion in Harold Monro's survey *Some Contemporary Poets* (1920) indicates that she had gained some reputation as a poet by the 1920s. Her poems were included in *The Oxford Book of Modern Verse* (1936) and in several other anthologies in Britain and as far afield as Hungary and India. Throughout her life, individual poems were frequently printed and won prizes in periodicals with as wide and varying readerships as the *Listener*, *New Statesman and Nation*, *Time and Tide*, *Punch*, *Week-End Review* and *Horizon*. As a translator, she was admired by Stephen Spender and published translations of French and Russian poetry; she judged poetry competitions, gave lectures and readings in Cambridge, Edinburgh, London, and on BBC radio. Her *Collected*

Poems was third choice of the Poetry Society in 1954 and she was awarded the Queen's Medal for Poetry in 1959. Since her death, her poetry has been paid little attention, and little is written about her apart from what is recorded in her cousin Gwen Raverat's autobiographical *Period Piece: A Cambridge Childhood.*

An eclectic reader of both traditional and contemporary poetry, Frances Cornford was not, as has been suggested, ignorant of poetic fashions. She was her own most severe critic, counting her early poems as 'juvenilia . . . Kiplinesque and clichéd'.[1] She has wrongly been tethered to the Georgian school, probably on account of the encouragements from Edward Marsh and of her friendship with Rupert Brooke. In fact, she recognised in Brooke her own struggle to resist the Georgian metrics which had been 'well sunk into [her] generation's unconscious'.[2] She moved from this early metrical conformity to the freer verse and less insistent rhyming of the later poems. *Travelling Home* provoked the greatest amount of fan mail, largely for its haunting depictions of the Second World War. The title of Catherine Reilly's anthology of women's Second World War verse, *Chaos of the Night*, is taken from Frances Cornford's poem 'Autumn Blitz'. In *Collected Poems*, she selected what she considered to be the best from the previous volumes and made some revisions to earlier versions, arguably always for the better.

Frances Cornford lamented that anthologists were 'like sheep' and she wished to be disassociated from her best known poem, the early triolet 'To a Fat Lady seen from a Train'. In this and other poems, the naiveté of the narrator can be mistaken for the conceptual simplicity of the poet. Instead, the constructed innocence of the observer, like the child in 'Nurse', forces the reader to ask questions. Frances Cornford aimed to represent the stresses of a speaking voice and the voice itself represents the complex psyche which is explored in the poems. In 'Grand Ballet',[3] the retrospective psychological condition of the story-teller becomes the story's subject. Apparently, Frances Cornford often talked about this occasion when she had been with her husband to see the Russian Ballet dancer Nijinsky[4] at Covent Garden before the 1914–18 war, and feared, needlessly at that time, his impending death – he died in 1943. In the final part of the poem the speaker wonders what will happen to this memory when she dies. 'Grand Ballet', like 'Nurse'[5] and 'A Peasant Woman', is typical of the poet in presenting death and life as inevitable conjunctives. Throughout her work, Frances Cornford's preoccupations are with the fragility of human relationships, isolation and duty.

'On August the Thirteenth (at The Mount, Marsden, Bucks)' exposes the stylised manners of the place's inhabitants. The observer characteristically presents a dual perspective and a dialogue: the orderly lifestyle of the privileged is both appealing and off-puttingly stifling. Clockwork routine and inflexible conventionality is suggested in the mechanical diction and the precision of the metre: 'You had to go/Who always had to stay'. Repetition of 'had' questions obligation and suggests the differences in perception of duty: everything subsequently becomes a difference of perception, of 'seemliness'. To the unprivileged, geraniums, zinnias and currant roll can appear a 'contented glow', but to the duty-bound, they are symbols of restraint, 'geometrically right...correct and slow'. The particulars of time and place present a specificity which is intriguing, but they are fictional.

The paradoxical nature of duty, as both a security and a restraint, recurs in the portraits of women. The hint of humour in 'Ode on the Whole Duty Of Parents' might account for its popularity, but the surface buoyancy of the mother's public voice is presented as a strategy for concealing her underlying turbulence: the forced neatness of the rhythm and rhyming suggests that the expected role of the parent collides with her silenced creative impulses and urge for individual freedom. Gwen Raverat remembers Frances' own mother as being more comfortable with literature than with motherhood, and entries in Frances Cornford's journal are evidence that she herself sunk under the demands of bringing up a large family, particularly during the 1930s:

> constant ill health, exhaustion to be skilfully dodged ... just keeping my head above water ... mostly the sense of my being is a strain – hushed anxiety, depression, guilt, not keeping going as if in a beleaguered city.[6]

The last of three long bouts of depression, for which she was prescribed a rest-cure, lasted from 1934 to 1940.

The unsettling effect of these poems is in the evocation of mixed feelings. It is significant that the simultaneous desires for being needed and for independence are represented as common to the mother, the nurse, the countrywoman bereft of her husband and her children, and the unattached woman. Frances Cornford's poems, as her personality, were compassionate without being sentimental. Among her copious correspondence are several testimonies that reading her poems was like meeting a kindred spirit. Sylvia Townsend Warner noted her 'amplitude and profundity' and the poems enabled Naomi Mitchison to 'turn things over and see right through for a moment'.[7] The Woolfs published *Different Days* and Virginia wrote to the poet in 1923 and 1929 to encourage her to write more.[8] She, in her turn, admired Virginia Woolf's *A Room of One's Own* and noted the tremendous difficulties for women, who were rarely free, either financially or spiritually. She eschewed the 'dreadful term poetess' because of its pejorative associations; later, she recollected that of all professions, 'none requires the expense of spirit as domestic life does on a woman'.[9]

Further Reading

Jane Dowson, 'The Importance of Frances Cornford', *Charleston Magazine*, Spring 1994, pp. 10–14.

Gwen Raverat, *Period Piece: A Cambridge Childhood*, London, Faber, 1960.

Timothy Rogers, 'Frances Cornford 1886–1960', *London Magazine*, vol. 32, nos 5–6, August/September 1992, pp. 101–12.

Janet Todd, ed., entry on Frances Cornford, *British Women Writers: A Critical Guide*, New York, The Continuum Press Company, 1989.

Grand Ballet

I saw you dance that summer before the war.
One thunderous night it was, at Covent Garden,
When we, who walked, beneath the weighted trees,
Hot metropolitan pavements, might have smelt
5   Blood in the dust, and heard the traffic's cry
Ceaseless and savage like a prophecy.

As by a sunrise sea I saw you stand,
Your sylphides round you on the timeless strand,
White, pure, delicious poised butterflies,
10   The early nineteenth century in their eyes,
And Chopin ready for their silver toes.
(O sighs unsatisfied, and one red rose!)

The fountain, of all movement ready to flow
Seemed prisoned in your entranced body. So
15   You stood, their Prince, most elegantly fair,
Swan-sleeved, black-jacketed, with falling hair
And hands half-raised in ravishment. O there,
Your Grecian arrow fitted to the bow,
You beech-tree in a legendary wood,
20   You panther in a velvet bolero,
There you for one immortal moment stood –

One moment like a wave before it flows,
Frozen in perfectness. Then one hand rose
And tossed a silver curl, demurely light
25   (O grace, O rose, O Chopin and all delight),
And the enchantment broke.

          That thunderous night
We saw Nijinsky dance.
          Thereafter fell
On the awaiting world the powers of Hell,
Chaos, and irremediable pain;
30   And utter darkness on your empty brain,
Not even grief to say, No more, no more.

But tell me, when my mortal memories wane
As death draws near, and peace is mine and pardon,
Where will it like an escaped dove repair?
35   To what Platonic happy heaven – where? –
Untouchable by Fate and free of Time,
That one immortal moment of the mime
We saw Nijinsky dance at Covent Garden?

On August the Thirteenth

(AT THE MOUNT, MARSDEN, BUCKS)

Out of this seemliness, this solid order,
At half-past four to-day,
When down below
Geraniums were bright
5   In the contented glow,
Whilst Williams planted seedlings all about,
Supremely geometrically right
In your herbaceous border,
You had to go
10 Who always liked to stay.
Before Louisa sliced the currant roll,
And re-arranged the zinnias in the bowl,
All in a rhythm reachless by modernity,
Correct and slow,
15 And brought the tea and tray,
At half-past four on Friday you went out:
To the unseemly, seemly,
Dateless, whole
Light of Eternity
You went away.

Ode on the Whole Duty Of Parents

The spirits of children are remote and wise,
They must go free
Like fishes in the sea
Or starlings in the skies,
5   Whilst you remain
The shore where casually they come again.

[47]

But when there falls the stalking shade of fear,
You must be suddenly near,
You, the unstable, must become a tree
10   In whose unending heights of flowering green
Hangs every fruit that grows, with silver bells;
Where heart-distracting magic birds are seen
And all the things a fairy-story tells;
Though still you should possess
15   Roots that go deep in ordinary earth, .
And strong consoling bark
To love and to caress.

Last, when at dark
Safe on the pillow lies an up-gazing head
20   And drinking holy eyes
Are fixed on you,
When, from behind them, questions come to birth
Insistently,
On all the things that you have ever said
25   Of suns and snakes and parallelograms and flies,
And whether these are true,
Then for a while you'll need to be no more
That sheltering shore
Or legendary tree in safety spread,
30   No, then you must put on
The robes of Solomon,
Or simply be
Sir Isaac Newton sitting on the bed.

Nurse

I cannot but believe, though you were dead,
Lying stone still, and I came in and said
(Having been out perhaps in storm and rain): –
'O dear, O look, I have torn my skirt again',
5   That you would rise with the old simple ease,
And say, 'Yes, child', and come to me.
                                          And there
In your white crackling apron, on your knees,
With your quick hands, rough with the washing up
Of every separate tended spoon and cup,

10 And with bent head, coiled with the happy hair
Your own child should have pulled for you (But no,
Your child who might have been, you did not bear,
Because the bottomless riches of your care
Were all for us) you would mend and heal my tear –
15 Mend, touch and heal; and stitching all the while,
Your cotton on your lap, look up and show
The sudden light perpetual of your smile –

And only then, you dear one, being dead
Go back and lie, like stone, upon your bed.

A Peasant Woman

I saw you sit waiting with your sewing on your knees,
Till a man should claim the comfort of your body
And your industry and presence for his own.

I saw you sit waiting with your sewing on your knees,
5 Till the child growing hidden in your body
Should become a living creature in the light.

I saw you sit waiting with your sewing on your knees,
Till your child who had ventured to the city
Should return to the shelter of his home.

10 I saw you sit waiting with your sewing on your knees
– Your unreturning son was in the city
Till Death should come along the cobbled street.

I saw you sit waiting with your sewing on your knees.

The Single Woman

Now quenched each midnight window is. Now unimpeded
    Darkness descends on roof and tree and slope;
And in my heart the houses that you have not needed
    Put out their lights of comfort and of hope. '

[49]

Notes

1 'Literary Memoirs and Memories', undated, *Literary Papers of Frances Cornford*, Add. Mss. 58384, London, British Library, Department of Manuscripts.
2 Frances Cornford, 'Notes for a Talk', undated, ibid., Add. Mss. 58385.
3 'Grand Ballet' was printed in *Time and Tide*, 12 March 1932.
4 Vaslev Nijinsky (1890–1950) was renowned for his sensational jump; in 1917 his career was tragically curtailed by insanity which was precipitated by his sensitivity to the horrors of war.
5 'Nurse' is revised as 'The Old Servant' in *Collected Poems*. I have preferred the original title and version from *Mountains and Molehills*.
6 Frances Cornford, Journal 1934, *Literary Papers*, Add. Mss. 58390.
7 Naomi Mitchison, (undated), 'Letters to Frances Cornford', ibid., Add. Mss. 58421–7.
8 See Jane Dowson, 'The Importance of Frances Cornford'.
9 Frances Cornford, 'Views and Recollections of a Sunday Poet', Tuesday 27 March 1956, *Literary Papers*, Add. Mss. 58387.

5
Nancy Cunard
1896–1965

1921   *Outlaws*, London, Elkin Mathews
1923   *Sublunary*, London, Hodder & Stoughton
1925   *Parallax*, London, Hogarth Press
1930   *Poems*, (*Two*) *1925*, London, Aquila Press
1934   *Negro: an anthology*, ed., London, Wishart & Co; New York, Frederick Ungar Publishing Co, 1970
1941   *Psalm of the Palms and Sonnets*, (unpublished)
1944   *Rélève into Marquis*, Derby, The Grasshopper Press
1944   *Poems for France*, ed., London, La France Libre
1949   *Poèmes à la France*, ed., Paris, Pierre Seghers
1958   *Sonnets on Spain*, (unpublished)

Born in Leicestershire, Nancy Cunard was the daughter of the American Maud Alice Burke and Sir Bach Cunard. She experienced the extravagance and elitism of the British upper class from her education at home and in exclusive schools in London and abroad. She rejected the safe wealth and respectability of her upbringing and moved to Paris in 1920 where she met Edith Sitwell and Anna Wickham, as well as Virginia and Leonard Woolf, Wyndham Lewis, Aldous Huxley, William Carlos Williams, T.S. Eliot, and Ezra Pound – who helped her to become a poet. Between 1930 and 1935 she travelled to America, Moscow and Geneva; journalists speculated about the motives and nature of her exploits, especially her visits to Harlem, and in 1932, she was the subject of scandal in the tabloid papers in New York and London. Undaunted, she continued to fight for the cause of the dispossessed; in 1936 she went to help the Republicans in Spain and in 1939 to give aid to the Spanish refugees as well as continuing to write articles on Spain for the *Manchester Guardian*.

    Sylvia Townsend Warner recorded Nancy Cunard's death as the end of 'a harsh breath of life, an embodied resistance'[1] and according to Samuel Putnam, 'Few persons have been more misunderstood than Nancy Cunard'.[2] Nancy Cunard published few of her own poems – most of her work was as an editor, publisher and political activist – and yet she is due proper recognition for her significance within the currents of literature and particularly for her contributions to our understanding of the Spanish Civil War. Seven of her earlier poems, including the title poem, were printed in the controversial anthology *Wheels* (1916) edited by Edith Sitwell; in the spring of 1928, she founded The Hours Press in order to help young poets and to promote contemporary poetry. She had associations through publishing with Laura Riding, whose work she also published, and through political activities she became a good friend of Sylvia Townsend Warner. She included poems by Sylvia Townsend Warner and Valentine Ackland in *Poems for France* which published dual language versions of all the contributions. Nancy Cunard herself was a meticulous translator and could work in several languages; she wrote poems in English, French and Spanish.

During the 1930s, Nancy Cunard became mythologised as a rebel for her 'almost frenetic involvement in social and political affairs'.[3] Her articles appeared in *Left Review* and the publication of her bold treatise *Black Man and White Ladyship* (1931) caused a stir in her own family and in the media; it was an attack on the prejudices of the British aristocracy which concluded with the words, 'How come, white man, is the rest of the world to be reformed in your dreary and decadent image?'[4] Her commitment to consciousness-raising concerning inequalities of class, sex and race had been born from the experiences of her travels and from her close friendship with the black musician Henry Crowder. Her anthology of negro writing was a landmark in its time. It was an eight hundred page 'record of the struggles and achievements, the persecutions and the revolts against them, of the Negro people' and consisted of writings and photographs which documented various phases of Negro life.[5] William Plomer attests that her negrophilism was 'passionately serious' and that 'its influence augmented other influences already at work ... [it was] ultimately of great political importance in the world.'[6]

Nancy Cunard is alleged to have instigated the letter from Paris addressed 'To the Writers and Poets of England, Scotland, Ireland and Wales', requesting statements of their position regarding the Spanish Civil War. Inevitably, she had a mixed response; amongst those who were prepared to profess their support for the Republicans were Valentine Ackland and Sylvia Townsend Warner whereas Vita Sackville-West was against 'subterranean forms of propaganda'. The replies were published by *Left Review*, in 1937, as 'Authors Take Sides on the Spanish War'[7] and sold a good 3, 000 copies.

Nancy Cunard's translations of Neruda and two of her poems are included in *The Penguin Book of Spanish Civil War Verse*. 'To Eat To-day' is dated Barcelona, September 13, 1938; it was printed in the *New Statesman and Nation*, 1 October 1938 and the final stanza in *Voice of Spain*, no. 1, January 1939. She is an example of how the Spanish War fuelled poetry 'as if a rock had been struck and a spring leapt out of it'.[8] On her second visit to Barcelona, she was appalled at the 'hunger everywhere' and started a food campaign through the *Manchester*

Guardian, News Chronicle and *Daily Herald.*[9] 'To Eat To-day' has a journalistic economy combined with the polemical tone of protest poetry; although the rhythms are ragged in places, the poem has striking aural and visual properties; the synchronic voices of observer and victim produce tonal resonances which support the filmic elements of the poem. The inclusion of Spanish phrases is an important strategy in disorientating the English reader who might otherwise have some psychological immunity to the images of the suffering peasants whose home has been bombed. It is one of several poems about the Spanish Civil War which Nancy Cunard had hoped would make up a volume but which she never completed.

Further Reading

Shari Benstock, ed., *Women of the Left Bank*, London, Virago, 1987.
Samuel Putnam, *Nancy Cunard: Brave Poet, Indomitable Rebel 1896–1965*, Philadelphia, Chilton Book Company, 1968.

To Eat To-day

They come without siren-song or any ushering
Over the usual street of man's middle day,
Come unbelievably – abstract – beyond human vision –
Codicils, dashes along the great Maniac speech.
5   "Helmeted Nuremberg, nothing," said the people of Barcelona,
The people of Spain – "Ya lo sabemos, we have suffered all."

Gangrene of German cross, you sirs in the ether,
Sons of Romulus, Wotan – is the mark worth the bomb?
What was in it? salt and a half-pint of olive,
10   Nothing else but the woman, she treasured it terribly,
Oil, for the day folks would come, refugees from Levante,
Maybe with greens . . . one round meal – but you killed her,
Killed four children outside, with the house, and the pregnant cat.
Heil, hand of Rome, you passed – and that is all.

15   I wonder – do you eat before you do these things,
Is it a cocktail or is it a pousse-café?
Are you sitting at mess now, saying "visibility medium . . .
We got the port, or near it, with half-a-dozen," I wonder –
Or highing it yet, on the home-run to Mallorca,
20   Cold at 5000 up, cursing a jammed release . . .
"Give it 'em, puta Madonna, here, over Arenys –

Per Bacco, it's nearly two – bloody sandwich it's made down there –

[53]

Aren't we going to eat to-day, teniente? *te-niente?*"
Driver in the clouds fuming, fumbler unstrapping death.
25 You passed; hate traffics on; then the shadows fall.

On the simple earth
Five mouths less to feed to-night in Barcelona.
On the simple earth
Men tramping and raving on an edge of fear.
30 Another country arming, another and another behind it –
Europe's nerve strung like catapult, the cataclysm roaring and
      swelling . . .
But in Spain no Perhaps, and To-morrow – in Spain, it is, Here.

Notes

1 Sylvia Townsend Warner, 18 March 1965, *The Diaries of Sylvia Townsend Warner*, ed. Claire Harman, London, Chatto & Windus, 1994, p. 296.
2 Samuel Putnam, *Nancy Cunard*, p. 101.
3 Hugh Ford, in Samuel Putnam, *Nancy Cunard*, p. 37.
4 Nancy Cunard, *Black Man and White Ladyship*, in Samuel Putnam, *Nancy Cunard*, pp. 103–9.
5 Introduction to *Negro: An Anthology*, 1934.
6 William Plomer, 'In the Early Thirties', in Samuel Putnam, *Nancy Cunard*, pp. 124–6.
7 See Valentine Cunningham, Introduction to *The Penguin Book of Spanish Civil War Verse*, Harmondsworth, Penguin, 1980, p. 50.
8 John Lehmann; see Nan Green, 'Nancy Cunard and Spain', in Samuel Putnam, *Nancy Cunard*, pp. 171–2.
9 See 'The Refugees at Perpignan, Miss Cunard's Appeal', in Samuel Putnam, *Nancy Cunard*, p. 196.

6
Elizabeth Daryush
1887–1977

1930 *Verses*, Oxford, Oxford University Press
1932 *Verses: Second Book*, Oxford, Oxford University Press
1933 *Verses: Third Book*, Oxford, Oxford University Press
1934 *Verses: Fourth Book*, Oxford, Oxford University Press
1935 *Poems*, London, Macmillan
1936 *The Last Man and Other Verses*, Oxford, Oxford University Press
1938 *Verses: Sixth Book*, Oxford, Oxford University Press
1948 *Selected Poems*, ed. Yvor Winters, New York, Swallow Press
1971 *Verses: Seventh Book*, ed. Roy Fuller, Manchester, Carcanet
1972 *Selected Poems by Elizabeth Daryush from Verses I–VI*, Manchester, Carcanet
1976 *Elizabeth Daryush: Collected Poems*, ed. Donald Davie, Manchester, Carcanet

Educated privately in Berkshire and Oxford, Elizabeth Daryush married Ali Akbar, a Persian government official, in 1926. They chose not to have children. They spent three years in Persia until his ill health caused them to return to England. From 1929, they lived in Boars Hill, Oxford. She was described by Vita-Sackville West, whom she met in Persia, as having 'square red hair and a square white face'.[1]

Elizabeth Daryush studied and translated Persian poetry, but it is her impact on British and American poetry which has been most overlooked. She suppressed the first three books which were written before 1930, and the 1930s was her most productive decade, during which she published a new volume almost annually. Yvor Winters identifies the peak of her career as *Verses: Third Book* and locates the development and discovery of her talents to the death of her father Robert Bridges, in 1930.[2] As Poet Laureate since 1912, his status and limited theories of syllabic metre had probably restricted her experimentation. Roy Fuller discovered Elizabeth Daryush when preparing for a lecture on Marianne Moore. He noted the coincidence of their identical dates of birth and of their parallel poetic paths. Recognition of Elizabeth Daryush's metrical pioneering has generally been more consistent in America, where her poems have been included in many anthologies and received more serious attention than in Britain. In England, she was rescued from several years' silence by Michael Schmidt who published the last three editions, and whose commemorative poem pays tribute to her personal and professional qualities.[3]

Often, however, reviews of Elizabeth Daryush's poetry can read like school reports and the paternalistic approval can be off-putting for the first time reader. Praised for the 'outstanding qualities of the poet's diction; its quietness and concentration'[4] or as 'a poet of the highest seriousness',[5] it is understandable that feminists have been reluctant to claim her and she has mistakenly been dismissed as archaic. In fact, her irregularities and ellipses within the sonnet and other lyrical modes are strategies which illuminate the imperfection of experience and the deceiving harmonics of formal literary conventions. Admittedly, there is some nineteenth century diction, but the rebellious tone and the outspoken challenges to Edwardian respectability should counteract any assumptions that the poet is aesthetically or ideologically conservative.

In his Introduction to *Collected Poems*, Donald Davie aims to redress the imbalance of attention to Elizabeth Daryush's metres and focuses on her subject matter; he cites Yvor Winters' review in 1936: '[Elizabeth Daryush] appears to be increasingly conscious of social injustice, of the mass of human suffering', and comments, 'she had not lived through the first three-quarters of the twentieth century in England without registering and responding to the profound changes that have transformed the world of the English gentry which, as the daughter of Robert Bridges, she was born to.'[6] There has wrongly been assumed of the poet, a passivity suggested by the title of her best known poem 'Still Life'. The poise of the lines, however, deliberately presents the suffocating sphere of the heiress whose 'unopened future' suggests closure as much as promise. Sensitivity to class differences is suggested in 'Children of wealth' where the metrical dexterity constructs a sense of urgency:

> Go down, go out to elemental wrong,
> Waste your too round limbs, tan your skin too white;
> The glass of comfort, ignorance, seems strong.

The critique of social inequality and hypocrisy is remarkably candid in 'It is pleasant to hang out' where self-pleasing do-gooding – 'where your neighbours praise you no doubt' – is attacked.

The 'lovely nature poems'[7] are, in fact, disturbing depictions of human oppression and the elements operate as signifiers of subterranean anxiety and desire. 'Invalid Dawn' offers no rosy glow: far from transcending the industrialised world, it depicts the factory, station and hospital lights as emblems of slavery. As here, austerity, toil and gloom are frequently conjured. Duty is also a recurring concept – whether to parent and spouse, as in 'I am your mother',[8] or to principle; in 'Off Duty', the magnetic force of service which both attracts and repels is questioned. The voice in the poems often uses the vocative but the personae of both the speaker and addressee are usually unnamed and elusive: 'If your loved one prove unworthy, why then,/ by this much you're the freer'. The speaker in this poem dares to name the concept of a 'mistaken marriage' and by doing so again challenges assumptions about duty. Whether free choice is a genuine possibility for all within a class-ridden convention-bound society is the dilemma of 'You who are blest':

> You who are blest, say this: 'This canvas blank
> That's my free life; the years without one line
> Drawn on them of restraint . . .'[9]

Her evident preoccupation with the questions of freedom and identity and frequent images of enclosure can connect Elizabeth Daryush to the nineteenth century woman writer. Her poems are *about* acceptance and rebellion and do not constitute conformity. 'Anger', for example, confronts the impossibility of meek subjugation: 'Anger lay by me all night long'.[10]

Selected Poems contains what the poet most wished to preserve from the books of *Verses* I–VI. It includes her explanation of syllabic metre, given originally in the Preface to *Verses: Fourth Book*. 'If your loved one prove unworthy' is a characteristic experiment with a syllabic sonnet where she uses the 'stress laws as partly worked out by my father'.[11] Elizabeth Daryush was actually more adventurous than her father in trying to achieve a more natural rhythm; she never appears to be straight-jacketed by conventions of metre or form, but manipulates them. She used many five and sometimes four syllabled lines as well as blank verse. 'Still Life' is considered to be her greatest success with the 10 syllabled line. It is now commonplace to alternate between stressed and syllabic metre but it can be argued that Elizabeth Daryush paved the way for the metrical ranges of Auden and other poets who popularised syllabic metres after 1939. However, like Donald Davie, Peter Scupham regrets the over-emphasis on her syllabic measures and recommends attention to 'the total tone and effect of this enigmatic and rewarding writer'.[12] And she herself called strict syllable count, although essential, the 'merely lifeless shell of its more vital requirements.'[13]

Further Reading

Yvor Winters, 'Robert Bridges and Elizabeth Daryush', *American Review*, viii, no. 3, 1936–37, pp. 353–67, reprinted in Francis Murphy, ed. *Yvor Winters: Uncollected Essays and Reviews*, USA, Swallow Press, 1973; London, Allen Lane, 1974, pp. 271–83.

'Children of wealth'

logical

certainty

Children of wealth in your warm nursery,
Set in the cushioned window-seat to watch
The volleying snow, guarded invisibly
By the clear double pane through which no touch

closeted
ignorant

5   Untimely penetrates, you cannot tell   *oblivious*
What winter means; its cruel truths to you
Are only sound and sight; your citadel   *ignorance*
Is safe from feeling, and from knowledge too.

illogical →

Go down, go out to elemental wrong,
10 Waste your too round limbs, tan your skin too white;
The glass of comfort, ignorance, seems strong
Today, and yet perhaps this very night

You'll wake to horror's wrecking fire – your home
Is wired within for this, in every room.

Still-Life

Through the open French window the warm sun
lights up the polished breakfast-table, laid
round a bowl of crimson roses, for one –
a service of Worcester porcelain, arrayed
5 near it a melon, peaches, figs, small hot
rolls in a napkin, fairy rack of toast,
butter in ice, high silver coffee pot,
and, heaped on a salver, the morning's post.

She comes over the lawn, the young heiress,
10 from her early walk in her garden-wood   *upper class*
feeling that life's a table set to bless
her delicate desires with all that's good,

that even the unopened future lies
like a love-letter, full of sweet surprise.   *irony*

'You should at times go out'

You should at times go out
    from where the faithful kneel,
visit the slums of doubt
    and feel what the lost feel;

5   you should at times walk on,
    away from your friends' ways,
go where the scorned have gone,
    pass beyond blame and praise;

and at times you should quit
10   (ah yes) your sunny home,
sadly awhile should sit,
    even, in wrong's dark room,

or ever, suddenly
    by simple bliss betrayed,
15   you shall be forced to flee,
    unloved, alone, afraid.

'It is pleasant to hang out'

For –

It is pleasant to hang out
this sign at your open gate:
'Succour for the desolate' –
5   your neighbours praise you, no doubt;

but woe to whoe'er in need
at the inner door has knocked,
found the snugroom barred and locked
where alone you fatly feed.

Invalid Dawn

Above the grey down
    gather, wan, the glows;
relieved by leaden
    gleams a star gang goes;

5   in the dark valley
         here and there enters
    a spark, laggardly,
         to the faint watchers

    that were there all night –
10   factory, station
    and hospital light.
         Tired of lamp, star, sun,

    bound to my strait bed
         uncurtained, I see
15   heaven itself law-led,
         earth in slavery.

Off Duty

[handwritten annotation: sense of duty – role of women to nature]

The long low ward, now tidy for the night
Is dark but for the central shaded light
At the night-nurse's table, where, before
She goes off duty, the last day-nurse kneels,
5   Reading the prayers – a young probationer,
Tired to nerve-numbness, mind-stiffened, heart-sore,
After her sixteen hours' day of diverse
Toils, shocks, dilemmas, failures ... now she feels
The bonds dissolve, day-grief releasing her ...
10   She rises, says: 'Goodnight, all' ... 'Goodnight, nurse',
Sounds from bed after bed – voices or small,
Pain shrunken, or themselves again, but all
Made gentle for her. She goes slowly to the door –
Feels at each freeing step a check, a wrench ... What chain
Still binds her, draws her spirit back, back, to the place of strain?

[handwritten annotation: unable to leave]

'If your loved one prove unworthy, why then'

    For –

If your loved one prove unworthy, why then,
by this much you're the freer: if the block
to which you're bolted warp and shrink away,
5   why then, it only gives you further play,
makes life rough for you, of course, with its knock

[60]

and rattle, with defection's loud sudden
jars, but your own quiet integrity,
tried thus the more, has but more room to be.

10   So says one truth, but soon says another:
Now in your soul-tissues a wrong sap stains
the white rose that you were; your heart sustains
the wild-thorn traits of your grafted partner:
when the mistaken marriage mortifies,
it's your own branch and stem and root that dies.

Notes

1 Vita Sackville-West, 9 March 1926, *The Letters of Vita Sackville-West and Virginia Woolf*, eds. Louise de Salvo and Mitchell A. Leaska, London, Hutchens, 1984, p. 124.
2 Yvor Winters, 'Robert Bridges and Elizabeth Daryush', p. 272.
3 Michael Schmidt, 'For Elizabeth Daryush', *PN Review* 62, vol. 14, no. 6, 1988, p. 44.
4 Yvor Winters, *SP*, 1948, p. xiii.
5 Roy Fuller, Preface to *Verses: Seventh Book*.
6 Donald Davie, 'The Poetry of Elizabeth Daryush', Introduction to *CP*, 1976, p. 14.
7 ibid.
8 *CP*, p. 53.
9 *SP*, 1972, p. 34; from *The Last Man and Other Verses*, 1936.
10 'Anger', from *The Last Man and Other Verses*, *SP*, 1972, p. 14.
11 See Preface to *Verses: Fourth Book*, reprinted in *CP*, for Elizabeth Daryush's explanation on syllabic metre.
12 Peter Scupham, *TLS*, 11 February 1977, p. 146.
13 Elizabeth Daryush, *CP*, p. 24.

7
Winifred Holtby
1898–1935

1911   *My Garden and other Poems*, Scarborough, privately printed
1935   *The Frozen Earth and Other Poems*, London, Collins

Born in Yorkshire and educated at St Margaret's School, Scarborough, Winifred Holtby won a scholarship to Somerville College, Oxford in 1917, and left in 1918 in order to take an active part in the war. Tribute to her generosity, her activities and achievements are recorded by Vera Brittain in *Testament of Friendship*. She was an influential feminist who opposed the liberal tendencies of the 'new feminism'[1] and lectured on women's rights and pacifism. Her critical study of Virginia Woolf (1932) and her history of the women's movement, *Women in a Changing Civilisation* (1934), were commercial successes. She wrote some articles about gender inequalities and her letter to *Time and Tide* on the position of single women in society challenges both women and men to change the conditions which imposed financial dependence on the single woman;[2] she believed that inequality of the sexes mainly arose from a deep-seated conviction that women have less right to paid work than men. In the 1920s, she spent three months in central Europe and went to South Africa to fight for civil liberty. She became director of *Time and Tide*, and, according to Vera Brittain, *Time and Tide* became, like her work for Africa, one of those lifelong major activities which 'filled her thoughts and dominated her sky'.[3] In the 1930s, her energies were concentrated on *South Riding* which necessitated journeys to Yorkshire; the efforts to complete the novel sapped her time and strength, and aggravated her perpetual dilemma between being a writer and an active social reformer. She did, however, accompany Lady Rhondda, the owner of *Time and Tide*, to France and Germany in order to meet up with the Six Point Group which was working with the Equal Rights International for an international equal rights treaty. Although she had previously published several novels, *South Riding* assured her an enduring reputation as a novelist as well as a journalist.

From an early age, Winifred Holtby wrote numerous poems which she destroyed or left unfinished. The posthumous collection was compiled by Vera Brittain, mainly from those preserved through publication in Oxford periodicals and London newspapers such as *Country Life*, *Time and Tide*, and the *Observer*, and in anthologies like Thomas Moult's *Best Poetry* series. Six of the ten poems in *The Frozen Earth and Other Poems* were written in the 1920s; the three included here date from 1930 until her death.[4]

'The Man Who Hated the Spring' opposes the overweening attempt to subdue nature for the purposes of industrial progress. 'Trains in France' (1931) was inspired by a journey home from the French Riviera which reminded her of her VAD experiences in the First World War. Her squadron had spent the night in a goods van in a railway siding in Boulogne. The sounds of the passing trains became a waking dream in which she feared for the safety of her beloved friend Bill and others. The nightmare quality is constructed through the intersection of remembrance and premonition: the rhythm of the train's movements connects with the machines of war. This haunting by memories of the First World War was common to women like Vera Brittain and Winifred Holtby who had participated in it and who became a group apart from the academics who had remained distant from the action; they also felt estranged from the younger generation of intellectuals for whom it was only history.[5]

Winifred Holtby's poems tend to rely on traditional forms within which to reflect upon personal experience or to protest against events; loss and death are recurring threads and there appears to be something cathartic in the self-expression. 'For the Ghost of Elinor Wylie' was written at the onset of Winifred Holtby's four year fatal illness; the whole poem consists of three parts (part one only included here) – 'i Escort'; 'ii Coronation', 'iii Peace' – which correspond to the stages of her condition: anguish, turmoil and rest. The poem records her interest in the American poet who had died in 1928 from a disease similar to her own. She was also attracted to the rebellious spirit of Elinor Wylie who had lived a life of conformity to social convention until she eloped with an older married man. The scandal had followed them to England where Elinor Wylie began to write poetry. Winifred Holtby's poem was first printed in *Time and Tide* on 16 December 1933, and then reprinted, as an obituary, on 5 October 1935. 'Resurrection' resembles an early poem of the First World War in its meditation on the nobility of sacrifice: it was printed in *Time and Tide* for Easter, 1936. It suggests something of Winifred Holtby's lifelong fluctuations between faith and doubt concerning the Christian creed; it may also be an attempt to hope for a life beyond the death which she was approaching.

Her poems about women have a more marked contemporary idiom. 'Beauty, the Lover's Gift' tells the story of the woman who makes herself physically alluring to please her lover, but when he wants her heart, it is too late: it has been superseded by the concentration on cosmetic appeal. 'Boats in the Bay' is another version of the not-waving-but-drowning condition which frequently occurs in poetry by women; it is typical in exaggerating the buoyancy of the public voice which conceals the overwhelming trouble which the speaker finds difficult to identify. Winifred Holtby, like many women, suffered from the tension between the sense of responsibility to change the world and their own private dissatisfactions, domestic frustrations and physical ailments. Much literature of the period is about these pressures which duty and altruism forbade women to confess.

Winifred Holtby's refusal to accept social and sexual inequalities connects her, by outlook, to Anna Wickham, Nancy Cunard, Naomi Mitchison, Sylvia Townsend Warner, Stevie Smith or Ruth Pitter. She could be speaking for them all when she wrote, 'I want there to be no more wars: I want people to recognise the human claims of negroes and Jews and women and all oppressed and humiliated creatures. I want a sort of bloodless revolution.'[6]

Further Reading

Paul Berry, *Testament of a Generation: The Journalism of Vera Brittain and Winifred Holtby*, London, Virago, 1985.

Vera Brittain, *Testament of Experience: An Autobiographical Story of the Years 1925–1950*, London, Virago, 1979.

Vera Brittain, *Testament of Friendship*, London, Virago, 1980.

Winifred Holtby, *Letters to a Friend*, London, Collins, 1937.

The Man Who Hated the Spring

'A HITHERTO UNPUBLISHED POEM BY WINIFRED HOLTBY'

The man who hated the spring was cold and narrow,
    cold as water and narrow as a steel blade.
The wild white flowered dead-nettle, honey lipped,
The clinging goose grass, the gross and squatting dock,
5   These were his enemies,
    He could not bear them.
Wrens in the hedge, the silent groping mole,
The fierce upthrusting spears of daffodil,
    Mocked him and outraged him; alone, aloof,
10 Adding his figures, measuring his plans,
    He moved, invulnerable and austere,
    Against the splendid chaos of the Spring.

So he planned roads and villas and a race track.
I will harness the Spring, he cried, I will crush it down
15 And his cranes towered to heaven, his drills devoured,
They tore great wounds from the hill, great holes in the plain.
With cement, with asphalt, with stone, with lime and with iron,
He bound and ground and subdued and crushed the Spring.

20 The starlings fled, and the moles no longer mated.
Away, away,
Flew the birds, the bees, and the unseen crawling things;
There was glass to glisten, there were poles to pierce the starlight,
There were light and music and engines and walls and men,
And the Spring? cried the man; the Spring is no longer here.

25 But he had roofed walls and bought walnut smiles and bath tubs,
Enamel, chromium, china, glass and tin.
There was a white door – to the Birth Control clinic,
And a blue door – to the ante-natal clinic,
And a bright green lawn alive with brown-limbed babies
30 In sunsuits of vivid scarlet and blue and gold.
Have you seen my Bobbie? My Lucy's cut her tooth.
The twins from Number Seven are doing well!
Darling, I love you! Little one, will you marry me?
At the Co-op. dance in Unity Hall I await my love.
35 Where bindweed and daisy and nettle are driven to exile,
The lobelia glows blue between the crazy pavements;
Love, locked out with the moles and the mice and the badgers,
Comes home at night with the corporation tram,
And the Spring, the Spring, crushed by cement and iron,
40 Mocks from the laughter of girls, the bleat of the saxophone,
In the hurried rush to the shop for a new pink petticoat –
The Spring, the Spring breaks through.

Time and Tide, 7 March 1936

Trains in France

All through the night among the unseen hills
    The trains,
The fire-eyed trains,
Call to each other their wild seeking cry.
5 And I,
Who thought I had forgotten all the War
Remember now a night in Camiers,
When, through the darkness, as I wakeful lay
    I heard the trains,
10   The savage, shrieking trains,
Call to each other their fierce hunting-cry,
Ruthless, inevitable, as the beasts
    After their prey.

Made for this end by their creators, they,
15   Whose business was to capture and devour
Flesh of our flesh, bone of our very bone.
      Hour after hour,
Angry and impotent I lay alone
Hearing them hunt you down, my dear, and you
20   Hearing them carry you away to die,
Trying to warn you of the beasts, the beasts!
Then, no, thought I;
So foul a dream as this cannot be true,
And calmed myself, hearing their cry no more.

25   Till, from the silence, broke a trembling roar,
And I heard, far away,
The growling thunder of their joyless feast –
The beasts had got you then, the beasts, the
      beasts –
      And knew
The nightmare true.

Beauty the Lover's Gift?

'BEAUTY THE LOVER'S GIFT? LORD;
WHAT IS A LOVER THAT IT CAN GIVE?'
(Millamant: *The Way of the World*)

Never mind now. You have done all that was needful;
You have given my eyes their blue and my hair its gold.
You have taught my body to move with a grace unheedful,
And I am beautiful now. I shall not grow old.

5   You have made me sure of myself, and I am grateful.
'I too was adored once' now, and once is enough.
Why should you look at me, then, as one grown hateful?
Why should your voice grow harsh and your gesture rough?

Have I not thanked you well for your gift of beauty?
10   See! I acknowledge it. I am your work of art.
You modelled this gold, this rose and this pearl to suit ye.
Is it my fault, if you say that I have no heart?

Did you teach my tongue to be kind and my fingers tender?
Did you ask me to spill my sweetness to quench your flame?

15   You cried to my lips, 'Be red!' to my hands, 'Be slender!'
They have obeyed. You have only yourself to blame.

Time and Tide, 8 July 1933

Boats in the Bay

I will take my trouble and wrap it in a blue handkerchief
And carry it down to the sea.
The sea is as smooth as silk, is as silent as glass;
It does not even whisper

5 Only the boats, rowed out by the girls in yellow
Ruffle its surface.
It is grey, not blue. It is flecked with boats like midges,
With happy people
Moving soundlessly over the level water.

10 I will take my trouble and drop it into the water
It is heavy as stone and smooth as a sea-washed pebble.
It will sink under the sea, and the happy people
Will row over it quietly, ruffling the clear water
Little dark boats like midges, skimming silently

15 Will pass backwards and forwards, the girls singing;
They will never know that they have sailed above sorrow.
Sink heavily and lie still, lie still my trouble.

Time and Tide, 18 February 1933

For the Ghost of Elinor Wylie

i ESCORT

Not when you glittered, royally attended,
   Gallant and debonaire.
By brilliant words and dancing mirth befriended
   I was not with you there

5 But roused by pain, in the abysmal hour
   When angry pulses leap,
And black blood lashes its frustrated power
   Against tall cliffs of sleep.

Then, when the hounds of fear sprang from the shadows,
10   In horror's hue and cry
Hot on your heels, through the grey morning meadows

Hunting you down to die;

Then, when you thought that there was none beside
    No prince nor poet near,
15   Only the silver sunrise to deride you
    And your pulsating fear;

Then, when you turned, by livid moonlight sickened,
    Seeking the hidden sign –
My breath it was upon your breath that quickened;
20   The fear, the pain, were mine.

Resurrection

He had been free.
He had looked into the clear face of death and known salvation
As a bather strips before diving he had stripped
Himself of desire, memory and sorrow.
5   He had stood poised above the lucid water,
The sea of oblivion spread itself before him,
The kingdoms of the world fell back behind him
Like a grey shadow, like a small wraith of smoke,
Their hopes, their powers, their pleasures, their excitement.

Time and Tide, 28 March 1936

Notes

1 The 'New Feminism' is explained by Rosalind Delmar in 'Afterword', Vera Brittain, *Testament of Friendship*, pp. 449–53. See also, for example, Winifred Holtby, 'Feminism Divided', *Time and Tide*, 26 July 1926, in which she accuses the New Feminists of digressing from the goal of equality in legislation which must precede all other reforms, and for being divisive.

2 Winifred Holtby, 'Tea-Table Sitters', *Time and Tide*, 31 December 1932. See Introduction.

3 Vera Brittain, *Testament of Friendship*, p. 265.

4 'Trains in France', 'The Ghost of Elinor Wylie' and 'Resurrection' are in *The Frozen Earth and Other Poems*.

5 See Vera Brittain, *Testament of Friendship*, p. 82.

6 Winifred Holtby, Letter to her mother, 1933, in *A Feminist Companion to English Literature*, eds, Blain *et al.*, London, Batsford, 1990, p. 535.

8
Sylvia Lynd
1888–1952

1916 *The Thrush and the Jay: Poems and Prose Sketches*, London, Constable & Co.
1920 *The Goldfinches: Poem*, London, R. Cobden-Sanderson
1928 *Selected Poems*, London, Ernest Benn
1931 *The Yellow Placard: Poems*, London, Victor Gollancz
1934 *The Enemies: Poems*, London, Dent
1945 *Collected Poems*, London, Macmillan

Sylvia Dryhurst was born in Hampstead and educated in London at King Alfred's School, the Slade School of Art and the Academy of Dramatic Art. She married Robert Lynd, literary editor of the *News Chronicle*, a radical liberal and anti-fascist paper, in 1909 – their children became members of the Hampstead communist party. Robert Lynd was a prolific writer and editor and Sylvia wrote essays, novels, short stories and critical reviews for magazines. She was reviewed in and was a reviewer for *Time and Tide*, she published the *Augustan Books of English Poetry* (London, Ernest Benn) and her poetry and prose were published in numerous anthologies and in periodicals.

Although Grigson's dismissal of her 'characteristic flight of lyrics'[1] was undeserved, Sylvia Lynd does retain aspects of orthodox Georgian metrics in her celebration of the English countryside. The fact that her poem 'Country Song'[2] was printed in *Time and Tide*, 5 July, 1930, suggests that such poetry evidently had some appeal in the early 1930s. Sylvia Lynd's novels are more unconventional and more obviously woman-centred than her poems, although 'The Solitary' is an evocative representation of how the unmarried woman felt estranged from social normality. 'Beauty and the Beast' was published in *Best Poetry*, 1931,[3] and in the *Week-End Review*, October 1931. It is surprisingly contemporary in its reworking of fairy tale in order to question its codes and assumptions about male and female relations.

The Solitary

This was her grief, that when the moon was full,
And earth lay drowned far down in beauty's pool,
She only, through that laving loveliness,
Of all earth's creatures went companionless.
5 With secret wooings recking not of her!
There every other in a warm content
Bright-eyed and silken coated courting went.
Rabbit and stoat, weasel and fox and hare
Had the wide world for bridal bed and lair –
10 Ah, not for her the silver grass, the grove
Bordered with shadow like the robe of love.

This was her grief, none stood with her to see
The moonlit apples rounded in the tree,
The stacks and stubble misted in a swoon
15 Of molten gold beneath the compelling moon;
That while the willow leaves caressed her hair
None stood with her the caverned dark to share,
While the leaves whispered softly leaf to leaf
Of lip pressed close to lip. This was her grief.

20 And ah, she cried, That I must live alone –
The song unsung, the blank uncarven stone,
The jewel lost forever in the well,
News that the runner, dying, did not tell.
I am a plough whose share is red with rust,
25 I am a harp whose gold is grey with dust,
I am a wisdom that no man will heed,
I am a garden that no hand will weed,
I am a ruined house, a disused way,
Silence, forgetfulness and dull decay –
30 Ah, what false steward took and set aside
This talent from love's treasury? she cried.

Beauty and the Beast

Beauty in your silent towers,
Tiptoeing from room to room,
What entangled thoughts were yours
Of happiness and doom?

5   Still to the Beast your lips said: No,
     And still towards your heart love pressed,
To compass reason's overthrow
     And glorify a beast.

Your fountains and your painted birds,
10   The sparkle of your jewelled trees,
Spoke they in vain with silent words
     Opposing constancies?

Did not the rose, the pretty rose,
     The simple rose your heart reprove,
15   That was the guerdon that you chose –
     Augured it such a love?

Your sisters chose a golden gown,
     A necklace of the ruby red,
But you were more exacting grown:
20   Bring me a rose, you said.

For that pale rose your father gave
     The dearest thing on earth he had
His honour and his life to save –
     You were the price he paid.

25   Princess of all the Fairy Tales
     Utterly faithful to your word,
Whose humble duty never fails
     Your father or your lord –

Was it all pleasure when the bells,
30   The fireworks and the joyful
Began, and gone were magic veils
     And silent mysteries?

And those deserted rooms you trod
     While fountains sparkled in the sun,
35   Were thronged with an obsequious crowd
     Chattering everyone?

And that strange Beast you met in fear
     And loved in secrecy and shame –
Was it so well when he, so dear,
     Became a Prince, and tame?

Notes

1 Geoffrey Grigson, Review of *The Enemies*, *Criterion*, vol. xiv, no. 54, October 1934, pp. 143–44.
2 *CP*, p. 25.
3 *Best Poetry*, ed. Thomas Moult, London, Jonathan Cape, 1932, p. 31.

9
Naomi Mitchison
b. 1897

1926   *The Laburnum Branch*, London, Jonathan Cape
1933   *The Delicate Fire, Short Stories and Poems*, London, Jonathan Cape
1939   *The Alban Goes Out*, poem, wood engravings by Gertrude Hermes, Harrow, Raven Press
1978   *The Cleansing of the Knife and Other Poems*, Edinburgh, Canongate

Born in Edinburgh on 1 November, into the prestigious Haldane family, Naomi Mitchison grew up in Scotland, Oxford and London. As the only girl at the Dragon School for Boys, Oxford, she experienced gender discrimination at a young age. Although the school gave her an equal grounding in the Classics and History, she was prohibited from sports and had to leave the school at the onset of menstruation. She was then taught at home by a governess and later became a Home Student at Oxford University until she left to become a VAD nurse in the First World War. The dualities of her upbringing gave her an unusual breadth of outlook and experience in some ways: she was brought up as a boy and was extremely close to her brother Jack, but she was also expected to develop the manners of the Edwardian lady; her father's family were strongly traditionalist and her mother raised the children as agnostics; politically, her mother was a Tory, and her father a Liberal. Naomi married Dick Mitchison in 1916 but practised and propounded an open marriage philosophy. In the late 1950s she became tribal mother to the Bakgatla of Botswana and considers her education of the tribal chief as the 'best thing I ever did'.

In addition to a three-part autobiography, Naomi Mitchison has published more than eighty books of poetry, short fiction, biography, children's books, travel writing, science fiction and historical novels and is best known for her historical-mythical romances. Although she became established as a novelist, her success was threatened by her activities as a socialist and feminist which provoked considerable aggravation from editors, outright censorship and detrimental prejudice in reviews. Nevertheless, she contributed regularly to newspapers in London and Scotland. She had numberless literary acquaintances including the Woolfs, Auden, Spender, Wyndham Lewis and Rebecca West and was a particularly good friend of Stevie Smith's towards the end of the 1930s. Naomi Mitchison and W.H. Auden corresponded about and exchanged their poems, but Auden, and especially his followers, discouraged her – 'I have many drawers full of poems [which] I felt shy about publishing after Wystan and his friends made fun of my writing.'[1] Individual poems were printed in journals but several remain uncollected and the many drawers full are as yet unpublished.

For Naomi Mitchison, the 1930s were particularly eventful. She had given birth to six children by 1933 – the eldest had contracted a fatal illness in 1927. Her father died in 1936, her Scottish aunt in 1937 and her last child after childbirth in 1939. In 1931, her 700 page quest novel *The Corn King and the Spring Queen* was published, and remarkably well received. She was also committed to active politics and went to Vienna in 1934 to provide aid to the social democrats after the killings and violations by the government. She aimed to promote socialist and feminist ideals through non-fictional writing and through the women's, peace and labour movements. She was commissioned by Faber to write *Comments on Birth Control* in 1930, and published *We Have Been Warned*, a novel 'about my own times' (1933), *The Moral Basis of Politics* (1938), *The Blood of the Martyrs* (1939), a modern political parable, and *The Kingdom of Heaven* (1939). Although she joined the Labour Party in 1930 and stood as Labour candidate for the Scottish Universities parliamentary seat in 1935, she discovered a contradiction between feminism and a socialism which would secure greater advantages for the ruling sex, and, like others, became disillusioned with socialist communism during the decade. 'To Some Young Communists from an Older Socialist' was printed in the first edition of *New Verse* in January 1933 and was a direct response to W.H. Auden's 'A Communist to others'; it suggests that the wisdom of those who had experienced the First World War was being discarded by the naïve idealisms of the new generation of allegedly left-wing agitators. At the onset of the Second World War, she settled in a house at Carradale, Kintyre and introduced her political ideals into the feudal traditions of the small Scottish community. Her long poem, *The Alban Goes Out*, an allegorical narrative about sea fishing, was allegedly read aloud to the local fishers in the evenings. A shorter poem, 'Eviction in the Hebrides', expresses her lifelong preoccupation with social injustice and anti-colonialism – it was printed in *Left Review* in 1937.[2]

In the 1920s, Naomi Mitchison had supported the modernist commitment to an art which should be uncontaminated by political or moral engagement, but became more in sympathy with the social realism of the new Thirties poetry and was involved in the anthropological-cum-artistic Mass Observation Movement of 1937. Like her male counterparts, Naomi Mitchison could exploit the creative potential of the slum areas, as in the poem 'The Scottish Renaissance', where she depicts the soul-destroying aspects of industrial developments whilst suggesting the potential for renewal:

Somewhere up grim stairs,
   Steep streets of fog-greased cobbles,
In harsh, empty closes with only a dog or child sobbing,
Somewhere among unrhythmic, shattering noises of tramways,
Or by cranes and dockyards, steel clanging and slamming,
Somewhere without colour, without beauty, without sunlight,

There is a thing being born as it was once in Florence.[3]

In her poetry, Naomi Mitchison seems to aim at resisting the polemical urge, in spite of the radical voice of her prose. The context of social injustice is the United States in '*Tennessee Snow*'. The decay of civilisation is obliquely suggested in the seeming innocence of the young beggar's need for food which is invisible to the good folks intent on 'Keeping the Highway Code'. Naomi Mitchison recalls composing the poem to the rhythm of her car's windscreen wipers. In 'Hartmanswillerkopf' the notion of young boys looking at First World War relics as curios, to them as mythical as medieval warfare, is an effective way of unsettling a false sense of global peace. 'Thinking of War' has a characteristic immediacy and a cumulative self-referentiality whereby images and rhythms become increasingly disconcerting. It records her observations of the Essex countryside when driving down from Scotland and also her sense of imminent war which is projected through images drawn from the First World War.

The poem on her baby's death in 1939 is typical of Naomi Mitchison's matter-of-fact treatment of emotion or violence; it places personal grief within the larger arena of another world war:

These twenty centuries of bourgeois bargaining,
Since Jesus, himself a Jew, saw through it, saw there must be
No scales of corn-growing justice, but only love,
Have left their mark on me.
Now I am trying to bargain, to say take her death, my grief,
But save me the others, from bombs, shells, from pandemic
Disease, save me children and husband,[4]

'The Midsummer Apple Tree' is one of the more vehement of her poems where inveterate masculinity is challenged. Irreverence for the traditional images of Eden and the apple is defiant as the images are transformed into symbols of sensuality. The sexual instinct is rewritten as pertaining equally to woman as to man, and as natural and instinctive, not as the original sin. The childlike logic is overlaid with the insistent voice of the comrade. Midsummer, with its associations of youthful release, was a day which Naomi Mitchison had always celebrated. Again, in 'The Unfertile Heart', natural impulses are not easily tamed. In 'Old Love and New Love' she uses role reversal to insert woman's sexual impulses. The tone is teasing and there is a carelessness in the movements of a dance which she had in mind. The more insidious implication is that all is not well and that a few kisses will not satisfy; the woman goes through the motions of love-making, but her mind is not married. The recurring suggestion is that women are as restless as men. The effectiveness of 'Woman Alone' is in its ambivalence: the mental separation of the woman is presented as both sad solitude and spiritual freedom.

'Dick and Colin at the Salmon Nets' again depicts separateness, but the mood is more wistful; instead of triumphalistic independence, there is a resignation to the apparent inevitability that men will congregate with men and that women must remain indoors 'with the children and books'. It echoes Mitchison's assertion that feminism's battles had not been won: 'actually nothing is settled, and the question of baby or not baby is at the bottom of almost everything.'5

Further Reading

Jill Benton, *Naomi Mitchison: a Biography*, London, Pandora, 1990.

Mary Chamberlain, ed., 'Naomi Mitchison talking with Alison Hennegan', *Writing Lives: Conversations between Women Writers*, London, Virago, 1988.

Naomi Mitchison, *All Change Here: Girlhood and Marriage*, London, Bodley Head, 1975.

——, *You May Well Ask: A Memoir 1920–40*, London, Victor Gollancz, 1979.

Donald A. Smith, *Possible Worlds: The Fiction of Naomi Mitchison*, Ph.D. Thesis, University of Edinburgh Library, 1982.

To Some Young Communists from an Older Socialist

Under the cold eyes, the cat eyes of those young,
This car, cutting corners, into the ditch slithers;
And the middle-aged, mucky, stained and strained dither,
Feeling themselves fools, watched, their war-scarred withers
    wrung.

5 So we say, won't you help with the car, wise ones we want to
    trust,
But they won't – why should they? – they will walk fiercely,
    singing, with friends:
No drugs for the old duds, nor care for dud cars not worth
    mending,
Leave it and walk, they say, that's good enough for us.

We try to, walk, warily re-adjusting wrenched sinews,

10 But oh it's too hard, comrades, we can't, you've killed us, we're
        dead and done.
    Leave us by road-sides, sunk, head in hands, it may be sunny,
    Dreaming no more of the dances that fairies in fields renew.

    As for the car, we don't care much, it had jolly gadgets,
    If someone finds and mends and drives it, we mustn't mind,
15 Nor that, hoping to help, with you to give and take kindness,
    We have been left to a fate worse than we once imagined.

    Tolerance and irony were the things we once hated.
    Now there is nothing but that – you've cornered, corralled the
        rest.
    Look, our car's luggage of high violent hopes is only socks and
        vests:
20 Kick them away, careless, marching, you and your mates.

    We who were young once in that war time, we are now not young
        but apart,
    Living with photos of friends, dead at Ypres or Menin,
    Remembering little of lies or truth perhaps defended;
    We were hit then in the head, but now, hopeless, in the heart.

                                New Verse, no. 1., January 1933

Thinking of War

    Driving through Essex I smell the wild privet and
    The dusty poppies in summer across the land.
    Here beside Colchester the strong sons of Cymbeline
    Were beaten in battle by Romans. And here the Queen
5   Boadicea came screaming and charging: killing, was herself killed:
    And the dry July ditches with British blood filled.
    Today, too, the roads are full of mud-green cars, uniformed men
    War Office lorries, grimmish, between Epping and fen.
    Squadrons of Stingers buzz through the high cirrhus, not hiding
10 Yet not inviting the aiming eyes' sliding.
    Under them Essex, a likely battlefield, lies spread,
    Smelling of wild privet and poppies and perhaps the dead.
    I have killed a young rabbit, cat-mangled; its shrill pain
    Smudges red streaks between objects and the perceiving brain.
15 Its blood smeared my fingers, as aborting blood,
    Or one's own child gutted and bombed, wormed through the bud.

    Things should be simple on summer Sundays, driving and

Smelling hedge blooms, sharp honey suckle, sweet bed-straw
    bland,
Wild roses ramping pale above hay-cocks,
20 Cherry bobs half-seen
Netted for markets. But the sons of Cymbeline,
Togodumnus and Caradoz, fought the legions, nor either escaped;
And the queen's little rabbit daughters were whipped and raped;
And the war-coloured lorries are coming, stringing along the
    roads,
25 Shockingly death intentioned; and their loads, baddish loads.
So now the wild privet and roses are abolished by the smell
Of the greased lorries churning up dust and dung. And all is not
    well.

Time and Tide, 10 October 1936

Hartmanswillerkopf

The barbed wire looks incredibly evil still.
Men were bleeding to death here twenty years ago:
Jolliment morts pour la patrie.
As I remember it, for years long life crowded under the wire,
5 Bleeding to death.
Doubtless the willow-herb came first.
Then came the saplings, alder, ash and willow,
Poisoned at first in shell holes, now more flourishing.
Next came the children, the boys, kind and embarrassed,
10 Interested certainly, as in the Moyennes Ages;
Dug-outs and arquebuses, trenches and boiling oil,
Machine gun emplacements, wire, bows and arrows:
Their war will be different.

Time and Tide, 22 June 1935

Tennessee Snow

Snow down, snow down, you little white flakes,
That turn to rain on the road,
Where the good folks drive through Tennessee
Keeping the Highway Code.

5 Oh aren't you cold, little beggar boy,
And isn't it cold today?

But why do you want a dime for a loaf
That's under the N.R.A?

'I'm a worker's kid from a pit-head shack,
10   Poor white in Tennessee:
Oh, President, call your eagle off
Before he sets on me!

We reckoned he'd made a good bird once,
Oh that we did allow:
15   But the bosses they fixed your eagle,
And he ain't no good bird now.'

Snow down on church and chapel and house,
Snow down on river and tree;
But keep your cold from the hungry folks
In the state of Tennessee.

Time and Tide, 21 September 1935

The Midsummer Apple Tree

Comrade, comrade, come away
Down to Midsummer apple bough
Who you are, I can scarcely say,
Only know you are here and now
5   Under the Midsummer Apple bough

Here's the apple for us to share
Under the Midsummer apple tree.
Priests and schools have said, beware,
Shame and sin and death, all three
10   Hang from the Midsummer apple tree

Comrade, comrade, these are lies!
Under the midsummer apple leaves
I can tell you and I am wise:
We are neither brutes nor thieves
15   Here in the Midsummer apple leaves

What we want we both shall get
Under the holy apple tree:
Eat our cake and have it yet,
Schools and priests must let us free,

[79]

20   All our devils be overset,
      Here where the hay is sweet and wet,
simple   I like you and you like me
      Under the Midsummer apple tree

Time and Tide, 1 July 1933

The Unfertile Heart

Rush fields can be made good by draining: dry hill pastures
Can be roughed up, coaxed into clover: manured and seeded;
Good bents instead of fesine. But the heart,
The unfertile, bracken-devoured gorse-prickled heart,
5   Deadened with rushes and hard nardus grass, growing nothing,
How can the heart be tilled?
Heart's pasture: Thames valley, Taunton vale cream-flowing,
Or tended sheep walks: yet for all that beats the heart's flock.
How then?
10   Lay the skilled plough on me, friends, dig ditches, tear with steel
      teeth
Matted and deadened surface. Burn gorse, scythe rush,
Rough up the stubborn heart. But then, but after,
The heart asks for its seeding.

Time and Tide, 11 September 1937

Old Love and New Love

My Love comes behind me
And he kisses me just where –
What has come in your minds now?
– Between neck and jersey
5   My bent neck is bare –
Are you thinking, are you thinking
That you might have been kinder?
– And I know that my hair
Curls a little, curls a little –
10   And your hands that remind me,
And your breath in my hair

My love comes behind me
And his lips are like bees –
What has come in my mind now?

15 – That light on the clover,
  That settle and tease –
  I am thinking, I am thinking,
  As my eyes look out blindly
  And I stiffen at the knees,
20 Of my new love, of my new love,
  Who is fonder and kinder
  And is far overseas.

       Time and Tide, 20 October 1934

[handwritten: Free verse – thoughts]

Woman Alone

[handwritten: conflict between duties as a wife & other outlets]

 A woman comforts a man, staring
 Beyond his pillowed head, thinking
 Of other things, of needful cooking and sewing,
 Of flowers in a vase, of the idea of God.
5 She is giving only her body.
 But the man is comforted, he does not know,
 Blinded by customary eyes, lips, breasts, tender hands,
 That woman's mind is faithless
 It is not with him
10 Nor with any man, for to her all men are children.

[handwritten: reason sibly]

 She has been sucked by baby men, giving them her body
 As now she gives it.
 Suckling, she thought of other things,
 Staring out gently over small, breast-pillowed heads, thinking
15 Of necessary things.
 Faithless *[handwritten: dissatisfied – wishes to escape her role]*
 The woman alone.

       Time and Tide, 7 December 1935

[handwritten: unable to go labour]

Dick and Colin at the Salmon Nets

Outside, in the arin, on the edge of evening,
 There are men netting salmon at the mouth of the Tweed;
Two men go out of the house to watch this thing,
 Down the steep banks and field tracks to their minds' and
  bodies' need.

5   How can I, being a woman, write all that down?
     How can I see the quiet pushing salmon against the net?
     How can I see behind the sticks and pipe-smoke, the intent frown,
     And the things speech cannot help with on which man's heart is
        set?

     Must we be apart always, you watching the salmon nets, you in
        the rain,
10   Thinking of love or politics or what I don't know,
     While I stay in with the children and books, and never again
        Haul with the men on the fish nets, or walking slow
     Through the wet grass in fields where horses have lain,
        Be as sure of my friends as I am of the long Tweed's flow?

Time and Tide, 25 February 1933

Notes

1 Jill Benton, *Naomi Mitchison*, p. 90.
2 'Eviction in the Hebrides', *Left Review*, vol. 3, no. 1, February 1937, p. 20.
3 'The Scottish Renaissance' was published in the *Modern Scot*, and other periodicals. See Jill Benton, *Naomi Mitchison*, p. 10.
4 'Clemency Ealasaid', *The Bull Calves*, London, Jonathan Cape, 1947; Glasgow, R. Drew, 1987. See Jill Benton, *Naomi Mitchison*, p. 122.
5 See Jill Benton, *Naomi Mitchison*, p. 72.

10
Ruth Pitter
1897–1992

1920   *First Poems*, London, Cecil Palmer

1927   *First and Second Poems*, Preface by Hilaire Belloc, London, Sheed & Ward

1931   *Persephone in Hades*, privately printed

1934   *A Mad Lady's Garland*, London, Cresset; New York, Macmillan

1936   *A Trophy of Arms: Poems 1926–1935*, London, Cresset; New York, Macmillan

1939   *The Spirit Watches*, London, Cresset; New York, Macmillan

1941   *The Rude Potato*, illustrated by Roger Furse, London, Cresset

1945   *The Bridge: Poems 1939–1944*, London, Cresset; New York, Macmillan

1946   *Pitter On Cats*, London, Cresset

1951   *Urania*, London, Cresset

1953   *The Ermine: Poems 1942–1952*, London, Cresset

1966   *Still By Choice*, London, Cresset

1968   *Poems 1926–1966*, London, Barrie & Rockliff

1969   *Ruth Pitter: Collected Poems*, New York, Macmillan

1975   *End of Drought*, London, Barrie & Jenkins

1987   *A Heaven to Find*, London, Enitharmon

Raised in Ilford, Essex, Ruth Pitter went to Goodmayes Elementary school, and later to Coborn School, Bow. Both parents were schoolteachers and she was brought up to love poetry and writing. She started at the University of London, but left to work in the War Office when the First World War began. She then worked for an arts and crafts firm and in the 1930s, with Kathleen O'Hara, started a successful crafts and furniture business of her own in Chelsea. Ruth Pitter's poetry was first published in the *New Age*, *New English Weekly* and other experimental English journals. It has been frequently anthologised and was most consistently popular during the Second World War. She won the Hawthornden Prize for the best imaginative work of the year with *A Trophy of*

Arms in 1937, the Heinemann Award for *The Ermine* (1953) and was the first woman to receive the Queen's Medal for Poetry in 1955. In 1974, Ruth Pitter received the C. Lit., the highest honour of the Royal Society of Literature, and in 1979, was awarded a CBE.

After she had won the Hawthornden Prize, she visited Vita Sackville-West who had presented it and who records her first impressions of Ruth Pitter, 'charming ... *real*, very intelligent, full of ideas. I have seldom got on so readily and easily with anyone'.[1] In contrast, Julian Symons condemned her prizewinning poems as 'completely artificial, imitative, dead'.[2] The dismissal might either suggest male jealousy or that she was a traditionalist and out of kilter with the modern world. It may be difficult to position Ruth Pitter according to identified poetic conventions, but she does not operate in ignorance of them. She was as conversant with the neo-Romantic poems of Dylan Thomas as with the modernist works of T.S. Eliot and the mixed climate of modern poetry suited her preference for stylistic independence. In 1936, James Stephens called her not a major or minor but a 'pure' poet, one who avoids siding with either 'intellection' or lay emotion.[3] She was, in fact, like her male contemporaries in that she 'maintained contact with natural speech and several centuries of poetic tradition.'[4]

A social conscience is expressed in her poetry, as in her life, by a 'compassion for small beasts, for old and battered people, for the sick at heart',[5] but she is never condescending towards the socially deprived. 'Old, Husbandless, Childless', celebrates the human spirit whilst lamenting the subject's misfortune. The poem illustrates her ability to depict beauty and fulfilment whilst being sensitive to 'pain, illimitable anguish and horror and ennui.'[6] The tonal levity or optimism, however, can be disconcerting and can seem incongruous with the commitment to 'capture some of the secret meanings which haunt life and language'.[7] The buoyancy or unexpected playfulness when responding to tragedy is a marked characteristic throughout the work, even before her conversion to Christianity in 1941. She deliberately deploys humour and popular forms like the ballad and narrative in order to engage the reader, but her intentions are serious. She thought that T.S. Eliot had been a disaster in making poetry elitist; she aimed to make poetry accessible to a wide audience.[8] 'Portrait of a Gentleman' is a mock-heroic portrait of the man who wants to get on and an implicit attack on the system which encourages social climbing. The seemingly innocuous 'Digdog' exposes the cowardly spirit of the English, fervently and vainly delving for peace where there is only 'dirt and darkness', 'dust and darkness'.

'1938' is another example of Ruth Pitter's insistence on combining the spirit of comedy with the material of tragedy in order to show their co-existence in a species which experiences both agony and enormous bliss.[9] The poet typically gives reasons for both despair and hope and also resists closure, believing that the mind rejects placebos: 'The earth is as fruitful as ever,/ ... but we/Have failed to love, and must perish.'

The narrative of 'Maternal Love Triumphant' both mocks and affirms the toils and sacrifices of motherhood. It is one of Ruth Pitter's several verse fables – ostensibly the song of the 'virtuous female spider' – and presents a topical dialectic about whether it is *nature's* or *convention's* way to couple: thus the basic fabric of the family unit is in question. The imagined rewards for mother love are called in doubt throughout, and explicitly by the parenthetical second voice: 'They'll do the same for me some day – / (Did someone say *Says You* ?)'. The suggestion is that personal fulfilment is a mythical construction of deceiving rhetoric. Another satiric narrative 'Ecclesiasticella: or The Church Mouse' similarly exposes the self-interested discourse of the wealthy who want to keep the poor content with economic disadvantage on earth by pointing them towards riches in Heaven:

> My name is poverty, my fame a sneer,
> For poor Ecclesiasticella's care
> Is nowise for this life which vanisheth;
> My riches be not here;

The poems here indicate the versatility for which Ruth Pitter has been admired. In her notes on her work, she lists her many 'applications of verse' from songs and satire to mnemonic.[10] The stretching of linguistic boundaries reflects her belief that the mind 'echoes far beyond its accustomed range'[11] and that through language we can discover ourselves creatures 'of a far greater range than we are commonly aware of'. She has been admired for the professionalism of her approach to verse writing and has been acclaimed by friends and critics who include Hilaire Belloc, Lord David Cecil, Elizabeth Jennings, Kathleen Raine and Siegfried Sassoon. The fact that her books of poems were published through six decades and that she enjoyed a late resurgence of praise, means that the Thirties generation of men did not have the final judgement.

Further Reading

Arthur Russell, ed., *Ruth Pitter: Homage to a Poet*, London, Rapp & Whiting, 1969.

Digdog

Inspired by the English of a Belgian hotel-keeper. 'Ze Ladies,
lof ze Griffon Bruxellois; mais moi, je prefere ze English digdog!
ze brave renardearther.' i.e. fox-terrier.

> Rooting in packingcase of
> dirty straw hurling
> lumps of it overboard moaning desire
> moaning desire of vermin lovely rat

5   ineffable mouse attar of felicity
BUT there is nothing
nothing but dirt and darkness
but strawdirt chaffdust smellillusion ALAS.
BRAVE CHIEN ANGLAIS
10   NOBLE RENARDEARTHER
DIGDOG

Alas! also
root in earth desiring
something for nothing digging down to peace.
15   Follow the mole and not the lark
bet with the bloke who knows
peace lies there whence from the dark
arise the lily and the rose,
peace rains down in rivers of gold
20   and there great nuggets of sleep
wait for the seeker ever been sold
sit on your tail and weep
for there is nothing
nothing but dust and darkness
25   but strawdirt chaffdust smellillusion ALAS.
LACHE ESPRIT ANGLAIS
POLTRON DE RENARDEARTHER
DIGDOG

Portrait of a Gentleman

*in business for himself in a small way and not doing too well
owing to trade depression and want of low qualities*

At the spraygun stands large heroic Ted.
The screech of air, the thunder of the fan
Beat in huge billows of din about his head.
But can affect no feature of the Man,
5   Who thinks 'This blasted stuff does go on thin',
But looks – this is your cue, I think, Miss Muse.
Mount the compressed air cylinder, and begin.
She from that vibrant rostrum frankly views
The face, the attitude, the matchless thews –
10   She from all little loves and passions free –
And opens thus. O godlike Ted! I see

On thy great breast the brazen harness glow,
On thy great shins behold the shining greaves,
Above thy countenance see the red plume blow,
15   The helm invisible, the sacred leaves.
Captain of all lost causes, and the head
Of fallen enterprise, I see thee stand
Like Alexander summoning his dead
Warriors about him in the spectral land.
20   Ah, should times mend, my Edward! thou wouldst fall
To sad vulgarity a sudden prey;
I see the Residence, the Car, and all
Thy wife's long dreams come true in dread array.
But ere the moment passes, let me say:
25   Ted in hard times is beautiful; he seems
Like Agamemnon, like the bird of Jove,
Like the great golden navy of my dreams
Manned by dear virtue and unbent by love,
Trampling down briny trouble; O that straight
30   We might beyond the raging of our fate
Cast anchor in the unimagined streams!

1938

O when will they let them love
As they are dying to do,
Men, creatures, brave spirits, friends,
The flower and the wonder of life?
5   They weep and die, and their bones
Mingle in earth, as never
In life could their aching minds,
Lost and parted, betrayed and forsaken!

They are shreds of a garment of gold
10   Flapping from many a thorn;
The sharp-edged fragments of a great vessel
That should be holding the wine;
The stones of a princely house,
Showing each some feature of grace,
15   But broken and scattered asunder,
The mortar being perished.

The greatest harvests of time –
Abundance, if fairly divided –

Are burned or thrown in the sea:
20 The mind, with its burden of love
Corrupting, now heavily weighs
The means of a myriad deaths.

The gentle are ground into earth
And the tender despised:
25 Honour's an ass-head, a bauble,
The mark of a profitless fool;
The good man's goal is the grave,
His secret longing extinction.

The numberless Warring voices
30 There keep unanimous silence,
The minds that conceived the slaughter
Are merged in harmless oblivion,
The hand that snatched up the weapon
Lies still, forgetting unkindness.

35 If only the grave can calm us:
If there my bones and my brother's
Lying in peace, united,
Bring no reproach on the mother
Nor stir the father to anger:

40 Let us go down together,
Having despaired of wisdom:
The earth is as fruitful as ever,
The sea still teeming with fishes,
The sun still lusty; but we
45 Have failed to love, and must perish.

Old, Childless, Husbandless

Old, childless, husbandless, bereaved, alone,
She knew more love than any I have known –

Familiar with the sickness at its worst,
She smiled at the old woman she had nursed
5 So long; whose bed she shared, that she might hear
The threadbare whisper in the night of fear.
She looked, and saw the change. The dying soul
Smiled her last thanks, and passed. Then Mary stole
About the room, and did what must be done,

10   Unwilling, kind heart, to call anyone,
      It was so late: all finished, down she lay
      Beside the dead, and calmly slept till day.

      Urania! what could child or husband be
      More than she had, to such a one as she?

Maternal Love Triumphant
or
Song of the Virtuous Female Spider

      Time was I had a tender heart,
      But time hath proved its foe;
      That tenderness did all depart,
      And it is better so;
5   For if it tender did remain
      How could I play my part,
      That must so many young sustain?
      Farewell the tender heart!

      A swain had I, a loving swain,
10   A spider neat and trim,
      Who used no little careful pain
      To make me dote on him.
      The fairest flies he brought to me,
      And first I showed disdain;
15   For lofty we must ever be
      To fix a loving swain.

      But soon I bowed to nature's ends
      And soon did wed my dear,
      For all at last to nature bends;
20   So in a corner near
      We fixed our web, and thought that love
      For toil would make amends;
      For so all creatures hope to prove
      Who bow to nature's ends.

25   Ere long the sorry scrawny flies
      For me could not suffice,
      So I prepared with streaming eyes
      My love to sacrifice.
      I ate him, and could not but feel

30   That I had been most wise;
       An hopeful mother needs a meal
       Of better meat than flies.

       My eggs I laid, and soon my young
       Did from the same creep out:
35   Like little cupids there they hung
       Or trundled round about;
       And when alarmed, like a soft ball
       They all together clung;
       Ah mothers! we are paid for all
40   Who watch our pretty young.

       For their sweet sake I do pursue
       And slay whate'er I see;
       Nothing's too much for me to do
       To feed my progeny;
45   They'll do the same for me some day –
       (Did someone say *Says You?*)
       So still I leap upon the prey
       And everything pursue.

       Two bluebottles that loved so dear
50   Fell in my web together;
       They prayed full fast and wept for fear,
       But I cared not a feather;
       Food I must have, and plenty too,
       That would my darlings rear,
55   So, thanking Heaven, I killed and slew
       The pair that loved so dear.

       But most do I delight to kill
       Those pretty silly things
       That do themselves with nectar fill
60   And wag their painted wings;
       For I above all folly hate
       That vain and wasted skill
       Which idle flowers would emulate;
       And so the fools I kill.

65   Confess I may some virtue claim,
       For all that I desire
       Is first an honest matron's name,
       Than which there is none higher;

And then my pretty children's good –
70   A wish that bears no blame;
These in my lonely widowhood
As virtues I may claim.

I look not here for my reward,
But recompense shall come
75   When from this toilsome life and hard
I seek a heavenly home;
Where in the mansions of the blest,
By earthly ills unmarred,
I'll meet again my Love, my best
80   And sole desired reward.

Notes

1 Vita Sackville-West, Victoria Glendinning, *Vita: The Life of Vita Sackville-West*, London, Weidenfeld & Nicolson, 1983, p. 288.
2 Julian Symons, Review of *A Trophy of Arms*, *Twentieth Century Verse* no. 2, March 1937, p. 36.
3 James Stephens, Introduction to *A Trophy of Arms*, p. xi.
4 Peter Dickinson, 'Ruth Pitter' (obituary), *Independent*, 2 March 1992, p. 14.
5 Comment of Ruth Pitter's award of the Queen's Medal for Poetry, *Observer*, 16 October 1955.
6 Ruth Pitter, Preface to *Poems*, 1968, p. xiii.
7 ibid., p. xi.
8 Peter Dickinson, *Independent*, 2 March 1992, p. 14.
9 Ruth Pitter, Preface to *Poems* 1968, p. xii.
10 ibid.
11 ibid.

II
Kathleen Raine
b. 1908

1943 *Stone and Flower 1935–1943*, London, Nicholas & Watson

1945 *Ecce Homo*, London, Enitharmon

1946 *Living in Time*, London, Editions Poetry

1949 *The Pythoness and Other Poems*, London, Hamish Hamilton

1952 *The Year One and Other Poems*, London, Hamish Hamilton

1956 *Collected Poems*, London, Hamish Hamilton

1965 *The Hollow Hill and Other Poems 1960–1964*, London, Hamish Hamilton

1968 *Ninfa Revisited*, London, Enitharmon

1968 *Six Dreams and Other Poems*, London, Enitharmon

1971 *The Lost Country*, Ireland, Dolmen and London, Hamish Hamilton

1972 *Sun and Shadow: Frederico Garcia Lorca*, translations, with R.M. Nadal, London, Enitharmon

1973 *On a Deserted Shore*, London, Hamish Hamilton

1977 *The Oval Portrait and Other Poems*, London, Enitharmon

1978 *15 Short Poems*, privately printed

1980 *The Oracle in the Heart and Other Poems 1975–1978*, Ireland, Dolmen

1981 *Collected Poems 1935–1980*, London, Allen & Unwin

1987 *The Presence Poems 1984–7*, Suffolk, Golgonooza

1988 *To the Sun*, Dorset, Words

Kathleen Raine attended state schools in Ilford, Essex and wanted to retreat from the 'horrific' urban background and rise above the socialist Methodism of her family. In order to arrive at a higher plane of experience, she converted to Roman Catholicism and, on winning a scholarship to Girton College, Cambridge in 1926, saw university as a gateway into cultural sanctuaries. Although her subject was Botany, and although she found it difficult to write at Cambridge, she imbibed the atmosphere of Yeats, Eliot and the Romantic Poets, finding the immediacy of Auden and Spender 'alien' to her.[1] Unlike them, she had roots in the lower middle classes, and so for her, poetry about the ills of economic dependence would have been writing out of her experiences rather than the opportunity for imaginative exploration. Although her early poems veered towards the mystical, she had poems published in the Cambridge magazine *Experiment*, she integrated socially with poets through her marriages to Hugh Sykes Davies and Charles Madge and mixed with the group of young Cambridge writers who included John Cornford and Julian Bell.

Kathleen Raine was as successful as any budding poet in having poems accepted by Geoffrey Grigson for *New Verse*. Consequently, she had a reputation established from the outset and was the only woman in the 1930s to receive serious attention as a poet. She took T.S. Eliot's advice and waited before publishing the first collection of her poems, but a variety, rather than the same handful, were anthologised and she had as many poems as any other successful poet published in *The Listener* as well as *New Verse*. She was represented in *The Year's Poetry* of 1938 with 'Desire', 'Passion' and 'Easter Poem', and in 1937 with 'Maternal Grief' and 'Fata Morgana'; these latter two poems were unusual in responding to current events and, significantly, they were the two most frequently printed in the 1930s. 'Fata Morgana' is a meditation on the Spanish War:

> While those were on the march to their desires
> Through painful brilliance of Iberian day
> Those arguing remained by their homefires
> Still living in the old unhealthy way.
>
> But I, who have no words, nor heart, nor name,
> Can still suppose how it would feel to march,
> Guided by stars along the roads of Spain
> Because of what I learn but cannot teach.[2]

Although Kathleen Raine dismisses her early work as youthful 'juvenilia', it shows her attempt to combine visual clarity with a visionary imagination which reaches beyond the material environment. In spite of her neo-platonic mysticism which accompanied her anti-materialism, she had a gift for precise observation, the qualities of a poet which were recommended by Geoffrey Grigson: 'report well; begin with objects and events; a stone begets vision'.[3]

The visionary aspect is effected by her use of mythological, Biblical and classical allusion. A.T. Tolley finds her symbols too persistently remote[4] and Adrian Caesar identifies her best poems as those where her use of elemental imagery – stars, water, wind – is tempered by metaphysical argument.[5] 'Still Life'[6] is one example, or 'The Fall', where the rhythms produce the kinetic energy of the 'ever-recurring forms of nature':[7]

> It is the fall, the eternal fall of water,
> of rock, of wounded birds and the wounded heart
> the waterfall of freedom.[8]

Of her contemporaries, she approved of Dylan Thomas, sharing his 'sense of the sacred'[9] and admired David Gascoyne for having 'nothing suburban in his imagination'.[10] She believed that a poem should awaken an imaginative experience and rejected the conversational tone because 'the voice of imagination is never ironic'.[11] For her success in the 1930s, with her preference for mystical writing, she could be placed within the current of 'dream-ridden' poetry of the decade; at the same time, she can demonstrate a stream of poetry which was independent. There is little recognition of the social or political climate, but she is at her best when personal and occasional or when human activity is the central concern:

> this is the day the cock crowed in,
> Crowed out the night; the lovers straying
> beyond the body's grasp, now must return
> each entering his dimension like a tomb.
>
> 'Good Friday'[12]

Kathleen Raine's critical writings are illuminating perceptions about other poets as well as herself; she has written her own biography and her own account of her work because she consistently wanted to be judged on her own terms: 'The measure by which I have judged my own poems is not one of comparison with others but applicable only to myself.'[13] She believes that her later poetry came 'full circle and rediscovered the power of ancient symbols'.[14] Her early and uncollected pieces are, therefore, all the more worthy of consideration for exemplifying her initial experiments.

Kathleen Raine's refusal to be included in a segregated volume may partly be a perception that the predominantly transcendental nature of her verse makes gender distinctions irrelevant; it also indicates the dilemma of the successful woman poet who suspects that her status may be undermined if sexual politics are believed to have priority over aesthetics. She has, however, an undeniable and formidable confidence in her own achievements which is debatably helpful to younger women poets and critics. There is a contradiction between her denunciation of the 'woman poet' as a valid category – one should be 'a poet, pure and simple'[15] – and her claims that 'men and women are different'[16] or that she herself is 'as good as any woman poet who's written in the English Language'.[17]

Further Reading

Muriel Bradbrook, '"The Lyf So Short, the Craft so Long to Learn": Poetry and Other works of Kathleen Raine', *Women and Literature 1779–1982: The Collected Papers of Muriel Bradbrook*, vol. 2, Sussex, Harvester, 1982, pp. 132–51.

Kathleen Raine, *Defending Ancient Springs*, Oxford, Oxford University Press, 1967.

——, Introduction to her poems in Jeni Couzyn, ed., *The Bloodaxe Book of Contemporary Women Poets*, Newcastle upon Tyne, Bloodaxe, 1985, pp. 57–72.

Notes

1 Kathleen Raine, *The Land Unknown*, 1975. See Adrian Caesar, *Dividing Lines: Poetry, Class and Ideology in the 1930s*, Manchester University Press, 1991, p. 138.

2 'Fata Morgana', *New Verse*, no. 25, May 1937, pp. 7–9.

3 Geoffrey Grigson, *New Verse: An Anthology*, London, Faber, 1939, p. 15.

4 A T. Tolley, *The Poetry of the Thirties*, London, Gollancz, 1975, p. 287.

5 Kathleen Raine, *Faces of Day and Night*, 1972. See Adrian Caesar, *Dividing Lines*, p. 137.

6 'Still Life', *Stone Flowers*, 1943, p. 56.

7 Kathleen Raine, 'On the Mythological', *Defending Ancient Springs*, p. 137.

8 'The Fall', printed in the *Listener*, 11 November 1938; *Stone and Flower*, p. 14.

9 *CP*, 1981, p. v.

10 *CP*, 1956, p. xiii.

11 'On the Symbol', *Defending Ancient Springs*, p. 121.

12 'Good Friday', *CP*, 1981, p. 5.

13 *CP*, 1954, p. xiii.

14 Kathleen Raine 'On the Mythological', *Defending Ancient Springs*, p. 137.

15 Kathleen Raine, Letter to Jane Dowson, 29 August 1992.

16 Kathleen Raine, 'A Passion for Poetry', Interview with Naim Attallah, *Guardian*, 23 March 1993, Section 2, pp. 2–3.

17 ibid.

12
Laura (Riding) Jackson
1901–1991

1926 *The Close Chaplet*, London, Hogarth; New York, Adelphi
1927 *Voltaire, A Biographical Fantasy*, London, Hogarth
1928 *Love as Love, Death as Death*, London, Seizin Press
1930 *Poems: A Joking Word*, London, Cape
1930 *Twenty Poems Less*, Paris, Hours Press
1930 *Though Gently*, Deya, Seizin Press
1931 *Laura and Francisca*, Deya, Seizin Press
1934 *Americans*, Los Angeles, Primavera Press
1933 *Poet: A Lying Word*, London, Arthur Barker
1933 *The Life of the Dead*, London, Arthur Barker
1938 *Collected Poems*, London, Cassell; New York, Random House
1970 *Selected Poems: In Five Sets*, London, Faber & Faber
1980 *The Poems of Laura Riding*, a new edition of the 1938 collection, Manchester, Carcanet
1992 *First Awakenings: The Early Poems*, eds. Elizabeth Friedmann, Alan J. Clark, Robert Nye, Manchester, Carcanet
1994 *A Selection of the Poems of Laura Riding*, ed. Robert Nye, Manchester, Carcanet

In accordance with Laura Riding's wishes, her poems cannot be included in this anthology. She was opposed to anthologies generally,[1] and, in particular, refused to be represented in women-only collections.[2] Editions of her poems are, however, separately available and she needs to be discussed for her involvement in British poetry in the 1930s, and because she has suffered from an over-emphasis on biography. She was evidently a powerful personality and where her participation in the literary world is acknowledged, it is often with mitigated deference, like Valentine Cunningham's dismissal, 'Laura Riding was, anyway, an American, even if we rank her at the ridiculously lofty level she induced Robert Graves to afford her.'[3] Her own retrospective stance was rather to insist upon *Graves'* dependence upon *her*. She was also later conscious of her reputation as 'a madwoman' or as having 'crippling mental artificialities'[4] and that critical attention had been 'shy ... with exceptions, both beautiful and ugly, and tending towards irrelevancy'.[5] Although she was respected in America,[6] criticism in Britain – where she was doubly displaced as a woman and a foreigner – has, for a long time, been sparse and elusive. Contemporaneous reviews started the trend of giving more attention to her personal myths than to her *writing*. Louis MacNeice dismissed her poems as 'appallingly bleak and jejune', suggesting that she try yoga.[7] Hugh Gordon Porteus, who begrudgingly conceded that her poems were 'good and no better', and valued *Collected Poems* for its self-revelations,[8] referred to her as a 'haughty and complex individual' and 'Poetess Laureate'.[9] Laura Riding sent letters to *Time and Tide* and *New Verse*, to counteract such personal attacks, but these exacerbated the name-calling game; Grigson printed one such letter under the title 'Sour Puss'.[10] Nevertheless, these antics do not comprise the whole picture: nine of her poems were included in *The Faber Book of Modern Verse* (1936) and Michael Roberts consulted her extensively during the formation of this influential anthology. There were also discerning reviews, such as Janet Adam Smith's in *The Criterion*: 'By her practice and influence, Miss Riding has helped several poets to write simply about abstractions, to avoid trivial decoration and irrelevant music, and to preserve the integrity of their words.'[11]

In the debate about whether she has been over- or under-estimated, A.T. Tolley supports her significance:

> In the Thirties, the Gravesians were a group apart, and have largely remained so. Considerably more important, though more pervasive, was the influence of Laura Riding. The impact of the sophistication of her language and rhythm is felt in Auden's early poetry, where her poems are directly imitated. Her work was clearly well-known to Louis MacNeice and to many others she was an important model.[12]

The 'many others' include British and American contemporaries such as Ronald Bottrall, Norman Cameron, Hart Crane, James Reeves and Allen Tate.[13]

In 1929, Laura Riding underwent a personal crisis, which culminated in a suicide attempt, but which was followed by a dramatic self-reconstruction. Her work in the early 1930s signals a revitalised search for a universal linguistic system. To this end, in 1935, she also began to work on *A Dictionary of Related Meanings* in order to give writers access to greater moral and intellectual vistas by extending their awareness of necessary interrelations between words. She seemed tireless as a writer of poems, stories, articles and letters, and in her efforts to create a community of fellow poet-seekers. She and Graves co-founded and co-operated their Seizin Press in London and later in Mallorca, and she founded the critical review *Epilogue* which ran from 1935 to 1938. Contributors were encouraged also to dedicate themselves to the purposes behind the biannual periodical. Its hardbound format was intended to preserve it for posterity and to foster the ideal of poetic permanence. Some younger writers appreciated her interest in their work, while others found her interventions excessive.

The long poem 'Laura and Francisca' (1931) is characteristic of her work in the decade in posing 'as many questions as answers':[14] 'My muse is I ... What shall we think?'.[15] The appearance of egocentricity and self-advertisement can be off-putting to the more reserved English reader, yet there is bravery in the self-doubt entailed in what was later explained by the poet as a genuine pilgrimage: 'My sincerity as a poet was a sincerity of spiritual literalness of faith in the truth-potentiality of words embodied in the spiritual creed of poetry.'[16] Thus, the apparent self-preoccupation can be justified by her belief that poetic utterance could express the universal mind. In *A Survey of Modernist Poetry*, (1927), she and Graves had defended the prerogative of poets to fabricate words in order to create and to communicate new insights. The poems in *Poet: A Lying Word*, however, express a growing disillusion with the ideal of poetic superiority: poems could not both use language naturally and lead the reader to a purer condition of mind. At times, she appears to anticipate the infinite circularity of the post-structuralist in dismantling her own discourse. Eventually, she found aspiration and practice – 'the creed and the craft' of poetry – impossible to reconcile: a realisation that crystallised only after her 1939 return to the United States from whence she had come in 1926. She did not, however, renounce her convictions, and dedicated the 1980 *Poems* to her husband of 1941, Schuyler Brinckerhoff Jackson, 'who knew and exerted himself to his extreme to serve the beneficent duty that words lay upon us.'

'Poems Continual' in *Collected Poems* are all from the 1930s. The poet 'dispensed with the literary conventionalities of poetic idiom' because these would compromise the diction of uncontaminated thought.[17] Poems like 'The Talking World' and 'Come, Words, Away' exercise this purity of diction, which was intended toward fulfilment of the spirit by taking the reader 'on and on, as far as poems could take' but which sometimes provoked the charge of obscurity.[18] Their individuality and avoidance of poetic conventions do make Laura Riding's poems difficult to assess. She uses repetition and assonance but rarely rhyme, symbol or metaphor; metrical arrangements can seem arbitrary and are variably fastidious. The frustration and the fascination of the poems are partly in the uncertainty of whether she is fully in control of her effects: 'We are undecided whether she is attempting to tell a truth or is pressing the fact that, through her chosen medium, it is impossible to tell the truth'.[19] In her later view, it is both and this tension accounts for the tonal vibrancy of the poems. Her own exact and exacting rationale as outlined in her 1938 Preface to *Collected Poems* is the most reliable criterion by which to evaluate her poetry.[20]

Her self-appraisals are realistic and self-knowledge is a thread throughout Riding's work, but there is a new detachment in the later poems. For readers who may elsewhere feel alienated by the puritanical austerity of style, 'Memories of Mortalities', an examination of childhood and childhood pain, is a secure entrance into her poetry. She is at her best on the subject of identity and in grounding the specific in order to lead to the general. Problems of language are here earthed in personal experience:

> But the world pressed a mirror on my shyness.
> 'Not shy' to the no one in that mirror
> I not self-recognised protested . . .[21]

Contemporary readers may construe this as the initiation of the child into language, drawing upon Lacanian theory of the infant's mirror phase. The prison-house of language is made explicit:

> I had learnt to be silent
> And yet to be.
> I had learnt how the world speaks.[22]

An interpretation of this repression as being specifically female could be reinforced by earlier poems like 'I Am' where she states, 'I am an indicated other', or her reference to the 'patriarchal leer' in 'Divestment of Beauty.'[23]

In 1934, in response to 'An Enquiry' in *New Verse*, Laura Riding professed a platonic attitude to relationships, a preference for spiritual rather than political pursuits, and pointed to a community of timeless poets as preferable to the homo-eroticism and communism of her male colleagues.[24] She was acutely conscious of gender distinctions and believed women to have a distinctive spiritual sensitivity.[25] In 1935 she wrote a historical study of womanhood, *The Word 'Woman'*.[26] Her refusal to be included in segregated collections is partly to avoid what she sees as their 'declassing' of woman poets.[27]

W.H. Auden's description of Laura Riding as 'the only living philosophical poet'[28] is a partial recognition of what Robert Fitzgerald identified as 'the country throughout [*Collected Poems*] is the country of the mind'.[29] It is perhaps as a poet of the mind that she is remarkable and it is her ideas which distinguish her from her contemporaries. In technique, however, Laura Riding was not out of tune with her time; her concern for combining a natural idiom with aesthetic purity was shared by most poets. In the competition between the goals of compression and completeness of expression, she achieved the syntactical economy to which many aspired. Her poetry is further evidence that form is not synonymous with ideology; although politically anti-left,[30] Laura Riding was one of the most adventurous stylistically.

Further Reading

Paul Auster, 'Truth, Beauty, Silence', *Ground Work*, London, Faber, 1990.
Deborah Baker, *In Extremis: The Life of Laura Riding*, London, Hamish Hamilton, 1993.
Alan J. Clark, 'Where Poetry Ends,' *PN Review* 22, vol. 8, no. 2, 1980.
Laura Riding and Robert Graves, *A Survey of Modernist Poetry*, London, Heinemann, 1927.

Laura (Riding) Jackson, 'An Autobiographical Summary', *PN Review* 97, vol. 20, no. 5, 1994, pp. 27–34.

Laura (Riding) Jackson; Alan J. Clark, 'RIDING, Laura', *Contemporary Poets*, London, St James Press, 2nd–5th editions, 1975–90.

Laura (Riding) Jackson; Elizabeth Friedmann; Robert Nye, 'Laura (Riding) Jackson at 90', *PN Review* 78, vol. 17, no. 4, 1991.

Laura (Riding) Jackson and Schuyler B. Jackson, *Rational Meaning: A New Foundation For The Definition Of Words*, previously unpublished, University of Virginia Press, forthcoming.

Laura (Riding) Jackson, *The Telling*, London, Athlone Press, 1972; reissue expected, Manchester, Carcanet, forthcoming.

Mark Jacobs, Review of *Selected Poems*, *PN Review* 15, vol. 7, no. 1, 1980.

James G. Southworth, *More Modern American Poets*, Oxford, Blackwell, 1954.

Notes

1 '*A Pamphlet against Anthologies*, Laura Riding and Robert Graves, London, Jonathan Cape, 1928.

2 *Poems*, 1980, p. 418.

3 Valentine Cunningham, *British Writers of the Thirties*, Oxford, Oxford University Press, 1988, p. 26.

4 *Poems*, 1980, p. 12.

5 *SP*, p. 16.

6 See, for example, Schuyler Jackson, *Time Magazine*, 26 December 1939, p. 41, or Robert Fitzgerald, Review of *CP*, *Kenyon Review*, vol. 1, no. 2, Spring 1939, pp. 341–45.

7 Louis MacNeice, Review of *The Life of the Dead*, *New Verse*, no. 6, December 1933, p. 18.

8 Hugh Gordon Porteus, 'Reading and Riding', Review of *CP*, *Twentieth Century Verse*, vol. 4, December 1938, pp. 130–32.

9 ibid.

10 *New Verse New Series*, vol. 1, January 1939, p. 30.

11 *The Criterion*, October 1958, pp. 113–15.

12 A. T. Tolley, *The Poetry of the Thirties*, London, Victor Gollancz, 1975, p. 38.

13 Riding contributed a poem-preface to Reeves' *The Natural Need* (1935); Bottrall dedicated his *The Turning Path* (1939) to her.

14 'As Many Questions as Answers' is the title of a poem. *SP*, p. 34.

15 *Poems*, 1980, p. 358.

16 ibid., p. 3.

17 ibid., p. 1.

18 ibid., p. 408.

19 Peter Jones, *Introduction to 50 American Poets*, London, Pan 1979, p. 224.

20 Preface to *CP* 1938 is reproduced in *Poems* 1980.

21 'Memories of Mortalities', *CP*, p. 261.

22 ibid., p. 273.

23 'I Am', *Poems*, 1980, p. 96; 'Divestment of Beauty', *Poems*, 1980, p. 267.
24 Geoffrey Grigson sent a list of six questions about the influence of Freud, philosophy, politics, poetic creed and customs to 40 poets, 20 of whom replied. The results were reported as 'An Enquiry' in *New Verse*, no. 11, October 1934. Laura Riding's reply is on pp. 2–5.
25 ibid.
26 *The Word 'Woman' and other Related Writings*, Manchester, Carcanet, 1993.
27 Laura Riding, Preface to *CP* 1938 in *Poems*, 1980, p. 418.
28 *Poems*, 1980, p. 410.
29 Robert Fitzgerald, *Kenyon Review*, p. 343.
30 Harry Kemp, Laura Riding, *The Left Heresy in Literature and Life*, London, Methuen, 1939.

13
Anne Ridler
b. 1912

1939 *Poems*, Oxford, Oxford University Press
1941 *A Dream Observed*, London, Poetry London
1943 *The Nine Bright Shiners*, London, Faber
1943 *Cain: A Play in Two Acts*, London, Nicholas and Watson
1946 *The Shadow Factory: A Nativity Play*, London, Faber
1950 *Henry Bly and other Plays*, London, Faber
1951 *The Golden Bird and Other Poems*, London, Faber
1956 *The Trial of Thomas Cranmer: A Play*, London, Faber
1959 *A Matter of Life and Death*, London, Faber
1961 *Selected Poems*, New York, Macmillan & Co.
1963 *Who is My Neighbour and How Bitter the Bread*, London, Faber
1972 *The Jesse Tree: a Masque*, London, The Lyrebird Press
1972 *Some Time After and Other Poems*, London, Faber
1976 *Italian Prospect: Six Poems*, Oxford, Perpetua
1980 *Dies Natalis: Poems of Birth and Infancy*, Oxford, Perpetua
1988 *New and Selected Poems*, London, Faber
1994 *Collected Poems*, Manchester, Carcanet

The daughter of H.C. Bradby, a housemaster at Rugby School, Anne Ridler was educated at Downe House School and at Kings College, London. She worked for Faber & Faber, as secretary to T.S. Eliot, from 1935 to 1940 and when war broke out she continued editorial work for the company. After the war, she and her husband, Vivian, moved to Oxford, where he became Printer to the University. They have four children and are still energetically writing, printing and entertaining.

In addition to her many collections of poetry and verse plays, Anne Ridler has written librettos, translated poetry, been a literary reviewer, edited poetry anthologies and introduced and edited selections by several poets, including Elizabeth Jennings, James Thomson, Charles Williams and Thomas Traherne. She contributed to the collaborative memoir *T.S. Eliot: A Study by Several Hands* and published *A Measure of English Poetry* – a compilation of her lectures on religious poetry, *The Four Quartets* and English prosody. Her poems were first printed in several periodicals, including *Purpose*, *The Listener*, *Horizon*, *Poetry London* and *New Statesman*. T.S. Eliot encouraged her to 'go on' writing and to publish her first collection. Her poetry has received favourable reports from writers as different as Julian Symons, Laurence Durrell and Nicholas Moore and her chief champion was G.S. Fraser. One of her most satisfactory poems, 'A Matter of Life and Death', was a prizewinner in the United States. Her poetry, particularly the poems of parting, was especially appreciated during the Second World War and *The Nine Bright Shiners* quickly sold out.

Anne Ridler is distinguished by being the only woman included by Robin Skelton in *Poetry of the Thirties* which contains three poems from *The Nine Bright Shiners*. She was certainly in sympathy with modern poetry: her supplement to *The Faber Book of Modern Verse* (1951) endorsed the anthology's aims of representing originality and novelty in order to register the importance of a new generation of poets and she worked with T.S. Eliot on *The Little Book of Modern Verse*, in which her poem 'A Letter' was included at the insistence of Eliot. Unaccountably, however, Anne Ridler has had an uneven reputation as a poet. Although always involved in literary circles, she has tended to promote the work of other poets without any self-advertisement. Initially, she found it difficult to be taken seriously as a poet, rather than as a 'woman poet'; latterly, her poems may not have seemed sufficiently feminine or radically feminist to qualify for a segregated woman's tradition – she is not in Fleur Adcock's or Linda France's anthologies of women's poetry, for example. On occasions, she has been labelled as a 'Christian poet' which may have carried associations of pre-First World War confidence or nineteenth-century dogmatism, even though the spirituality of her poems is never pious. It is the *discourses* of doctrines such as prayer which are explored in, for example, 'Prayer in a Pestilent Time', and which characteristically represent complex conditions of the mind. 'Now as Then' is one of the clearest representations of the nation's consciousness as it came to terms with a 'just war'. Published in 1939, it is a premature paradigm of Second World War poetry which interpreted events as emblems of innate, rather than social evil. 'At Christmas' is typical of the poet in using a specific occasion – here, the poet's first married Christmas, spent in the family home – to off-set a universal situation. Like many others, Anne Ridler's family had lost a son in the First World War and feared a repeat of history. 'A Mile from Eden' draws upon Biblical imagery of a fallen world in order to comprehend the second-time-around devastation.

Anne Ridler frequently articulates a mixture of doubt and faith which could be common to both men and women; in other poems, the seemingly easy profession of feeling marks her off as a woman and 'The Crab is In' boldly faces the aches and pangs of menstruation with characteristic directness and discretion. It also illustrates another characteristic which is the sense of the self as both observed and observer; it is seen most clearly in 'The Car At Night', written in the 1930s but not included here, and a later poem 'Mirror Image'.

In many poems, the modern world is presented as equally compelling and insidious. The contrast between rural tranquillity and accelerated industrialisation is presented in the frontispiece poem of this volume, 'Into the Whirlwind'[1] in which the scene-changes resemble the movements of a musical piece. Written retrospectively, it reproduces the rapid shift from peace and freedom to anxiety and imprisonment; it also captures the contrasts of prosperity and unemployment and the accompanying guilt for those who were comfortably off.

Some of her poems, other than those in *Poems* (1939) and *A Dream Observed* (1941), were written in the 1930s, and were included in later collections, although they had been published earlier in periodicals. During the decade itself, Anne Ridler felt hampered by prejudice from some male editors and critics. Like all the women, she was acutely aware of the movements of poetry and recalls a strong sense of Auden's influence on all young poets. Sometimes the shadows of Eliot and Auden can be perceived in her phrasing, but Anne Ridler's own poetic voice is distinctive in its balance of authority and modesty. The poet herself acknowledges a discernible development in her oeuvre towards a more consistently natural expression, although she judges the later control to be at the cost of her earlier lyricism.

Further Reading

Charles Brand, ed., *Ten Oxford Poets*, including Anne Ridler and E.J. Scovell, Oxford, 1978.
Anne Ridler, *A Measure of English Poetry*, Oxford, Perpetua, 1991.
The Critical Forum – Anne Ridler reads and speaks about her poems, Sussex, Norwich Tapes, 1982.

Now as Then

SEPTEMBER 1939

When under Edward or Henry the English armies
Whose battles are brocade to us and stiff in tapestries
On a green and curling sea set out for France,
The Holy Ghost moved the sails, the lance
5   Was hung with glory, and in all its sincerity
        Poets cried, 'God will grant to us the victory'.
For us, who by proxy inflicted gross oppression,
Among whom the humblest have some sins of omission,
War is not simple; in more or less degree
10   All are guilty, though some will suffer unjustly.
Can we say Mass to dedicate our bombs?

Yet those earlier English, for all their psalms,
Were marauders, had less provocation than we,
And the causes of war were as mixed and hard to see.
15 Yet since of two evils our victory would be the less,
And coming soon, leave some strength for peace,
Like Minot and the rest, groping we pray
        'Lord, turn us again, confer on us victory.'

Prayer in a Pestilent Time

Lord, for the year's apprehension,
    The soldier's dress, the civil pains,
And the expected cataclysm,
    Forgive, and deliver us from all our sins.

5 Now for the dread as darkness gathers,
    The lies like a gas that unseen burns,
For blindness, death and deprivation,
    Forgive, and deliver us from all our sins.

Deep our darkness, and powerless
10   Our love: to Thee, darker the shroud
Of flesh and more reduced the glory,
    For us a boy, and a malefactor dead.

Deeper the darkness, the light greater.
    Bring us where such light remains.
15 After our knowledge, weariness and grief
    Forgive us all, and deliver us from our sins.

At Christmas

'GOE SEES THE ANGRY KYNGES'
(Jasper Heywood)

Littered now the streets with light,
    tiddler's ground of gold and silver;
        but we pass the free grotto,
        pass the painter
5   chalking out our Christmas motto,
    till our present comes in sight.

Present time, though time's our gift.

[105]

Before the delectable joys,
    before the kind kings appear,
10   these to our eyes,
        thrones fierce and mean, show entire
the princedoms that our labours lift.

Their nursery faces much the same:
    Moloch with a dummy crown,
15   of our rage the real dragon,
    the ape of pain;
        these monuments of our private passion
as public tyrants have the blame.

Bombs will not bring removal.
20   But You who take the same journey
       as at this time, who seeing make
    them unseen, may
        make unreal their dreadful gate,
give us our star and our arrival.

A Mile from Eden

With buds embalmed alive in ice,
Flies in amber, the wood lies:
On snow even the shadows are white,
And we walk tipsy with too much light.
5   In slanting rays, like the damned
Our footsteps flame but make no sound.
While in this waste we wander
I tell him again of the godlike Flounder,
The garish desires of the fisherman's wife
10   (Desires we saw from the first unsafe,
For the same sin, though tropical,
Is in the Garden and the Fall).
But as I describe the granted glories,
The crowns, candles, golden floors,
15   I see his longing in his eyes:
Eyes of the humble hoping for Heaven,
Eyes of Adam a mile from Eden.
I see him a child with his joys round him,
One foot still on the coral strand,
20   The sun like a locket hung from his hand,
Now a man with his griefs about him.

If his hunger is holy, where hers was greed,
Can he always avoid the wish to be God?
Heaven revolves, distant, perfect,
25 Placid and impregnable as in a Collect;
And we walk in a waste of snows,
Yet see that power before our eyes
Which if we learn its usage can
Break up the amber, reverse the sun,
30 The bird's-eye glory to full sight
Bring, and outcasts into delight.

The Crab is In

The crab is in again, his monthly house
open and loth, patient only of force;
here he huddles on my back; the pools
that three weeks hid him, after the queasy pale
5 swept up my path before him, washed him to me.
Kings feeding fat, clogged rivers on the plain,
or choked with stars the dark, as all satiety
I feel him, clutching there, while each capacity
goes to enlarge him; dance the pincers of pain,
10 my self flies rook up to watch, afraid of the din,
sings to cover it, yet hears and rooted feels.

Any day beats by, force accepted, heals
nightly homing the Monday gloom of an office –
if you can say it heals that turns from brass
15 bitter to stealing hope in the mind a knowledge
in facts unchanged. So as with the anxious
this wasteful process can seem gentle to us,
flown out in peace all the disgust of blood and illness.
For we take comfort in any achievement, even a courage
20 that could not be refused: this inner success
may weight circumstance to temporary peace.
Even the periodic cancer need not distress us,
could we but keep the peace and lose the venomous.

Note

1 'Into the Whirlwind', is from *Some Time After and Other Poems*, 1972.

14
Vita Sackville-West
1892–1962

1917 *Poems of West and East*, London, Bodley Head
1921 *Orchard and Vineyard*, London, Bodley Head
1926 *The Land*, London, Heinemann
1929 *King's Daughter*, London, Hogarth
1931 *Sissinghurst*, London, Hogarth
1931 *Invitation to Cast out Care*, London, Faber
1931 *Rilke* (translations), London, Hogarth
1933 *Collected Poems*, London, Hogarth
1938 *Solitude*, London, Hogarth
1941 *Selected Poems*, London, Hogarth
1946 *The Garden*, London, Michael Joseph
1972 *Sissinghurst*, (reprint) Kent, Sissinghurst Castle,
      The National Trust

The life and loves of Vita Sackville-West have now been well documented; much of their curiosity value lies in her unorthodox marriage to Harold Nicolson in 1913 – in which they both practised bisexuality and had two sons, her connection to Virginia Woolf, and her complicated and clandestine affairs with other women. Her 'weakness'[1] for her own sex was exposed when she eloped with Violet Trefusis in 1920. There has generally been more attention to Vita's relationships, and thus to her letters, than to Vita herself or her books. Interest in her letters may also be out of a desire to 'read behind' her writing, as Virginia Woolf wished, in vain, to do with Vita's poems. In their day, Vita Sackville-West was more successful as a writer, in terms of her publishing record, than Virginia Woolf, although Virginia's influence on contemporary literature was apparently greater. Vita Sackville-West authored more than 40 books of poetry, fiction, travel writing, history and biography, including a biography of Aphra Behn (1927) whom she liked for her 'rakishness'. Vita was educated privately and in London; she travelled widely, often delivering lectures on literature; she was a reviewer and wrote gardening columns for newspapers and gave multifarious broadcasts on the radio, sometimes with her husband. It was her poetry, however, which she most valued and her biographer

Victoria Glendinning recommends that her poetry should be rescued from the relative obscurity into which it has fallen.[2]

Vita Sackville-West's hugely successful pastoral 'The Land', for which she was awarded the Hawthornden Prize in 1927, and for which she was considered as a possibility for the next poet laureate, has tended to place her within the literary establishment, and the poem's inclusion in James Reeves' anthology of Georgian Verse has relegated her to the unfashionable 'Georgian school'. Virginia Woolf encouraged her in what she wanted to be most of all, a 'good poet', by advising her to free up her technique, once she had shown that she could master it: 'the danger for you ... [is] your sense of tradition and all those words.'[3] In December 1928, Vita considered 'going into mourning for my dead muse' and was disillusioned with 'The Land' for being 'damned bad. Not a spark in it anywhere. Respectable but stodgy.'[4] She was similarly self-deprecating about *Collected Poems* – 'all that tripe ... I can't rid myself of the idea that it is all a little pretentious',[5] although it is likely that she was also hoping for Virginia's reassurance: 'It [*Collected Poems*] is the only book of mine I shall ever have minded about- (i.e. I don't give a damn for my novels, but I do give 1/2 a damn for my poems, which is not saying much)'.[6]

The description of *Collected Poems* as 'a frontier tower on the border of the land that we are leaving behind, that land is the England which is vanishing'[7] is more revealing about the conservatism of the reviewer than about the poetry. Similarly, 'Sissinghurst' can be mistakenly read and used as simple nostalgia for a mythical golden age. The actual regret of the poet is at having to leave her family seat at Knole in Kent which she could not inherit because she was a woman. In 1930, Vita and Harold bought Sissinghurst Castle to which they moved in 1932. In the poem, Sissinghurst Castle is a symbol of permanence and the poet ends with a refusal to weep for the past. Nevertheless, the mood is one of restlessness as much as of contentment. There is a strong sense of place in many poems, but place often denotes both security and restraint for Vita hated safety and mediocrity as much as change. Although rooted in English soil she could, and needed to, detach herself from it, psychologically, and literally through her travels. Her claim, 'I am content to leave the world awry/ (busy with politic perplexity,)' is echoed in her letters where she expresses her liking for solitude. Nevertheless, in looking at the 1930s, one popular image of Vita at her desk in her writing room in the Elizabethan tower at Sissinghurst, has to be tempered by an understanding of her addiction to adventure, and by images of her energetically extending the house and garden, her social engagements and her journeys to North America (1933), Italy (1934) and Algeria (1937).

The arrangement of *Collected Poems* is by subject matter, divided into 'In England', 'Abroad', 'People', 'Insurrection' and 'Love'. These wooden signposts endorse a perception of unadventurousness and they do not point to the variety of the poems nor to the treatment of the subjects; it is the psychological effect of the environment which is often the focus, and the unexpected disruptions to regular metrification support the poet's challenges to traditions. The poem 'Nostalgia' expresses 'love sickness' more than 'home sickness' – it is for her lovers, not her country, that she is wilting. She deflates the romantic images of both Persia and England – the pigeon towers are not squeaky clean but 'streaked white with dung, and goat kids born in blood'. In poems written in America, like 'In the Aquarium, San Francisco' and 'In New England' it is significant that it is the newer world which arouses her adulation. Any adherence to convention in her poetry is as much *stylistic* as ideological. 'To any M.F.H.' and 'Out with a Gun' oppose the fox-hunting of her aristocratic neighbours; there is a tenuous equation of the violation of blood sports with full scale war – 'Christ! has the world not pain enough'. Generally, however, there is a discomforting refusal to engage with social realities. She was self-confessing in her 'dislike for politics and a lack of interest in what must always be temporary' and recognised, regrettably, that she could not therefore get into gear with the poetry of 'Tom Eliot and the Stephen Spender-Auden school'.[8] All the same, Vita Sackville-West's attempts to get 'in gear' with rhythm is evident in the poems written during the 1930s.[9]

In her letters, Vita shows some consciousness of the disparity between privilege and poverty but is more affected by the competing pulls of the present and the past. The traditionalist part of her character was unable to embrace the modern world and yet she realised that conventions were obsolete. During the First World War she experienced some guilt at the misery of others, and undertook administrative work with the Women's Land Army during the Second World War. The poem 'September 1939' suggests some sensitivity towards the national situation, but it is her own crises which are represented in the brevity and the weary metre of the poem and which she records in her correspondence – 'I never felt so tired, physically and spiritually in all my life.'[10]

Between 1930 and 1939, Vita had expended herself in a network of female lovers. It is sexual rather than social politics which preoccupied her; in her female affairs she could, and did, exercise personal power. Perhaps her lifelong attractiveness to and conquests of women gave her confidence when writing about her own sex. Her self-explorations, albeit constructed, and portraits of women are her finest poems. It is tempting to assume that 'Valediction' is biographical in expressing regret at the fickleness of love and 'Solitude' reads like a private journal; it records the daily alterations of temper, but it also chronicles a life-span. It upset her female intimates with her seeming disregard for her 'cheap and easy loves', while her publisher, Leonard Woolf, considered 'Solitude' to be the best thing she had done. Even so, it cannot be taken as unguardedly confessional. She wrote 'diary poems' which were not intended for publication, whereas she had been working on and talking about 'Solitude' since 1927. This verse autobiography most expressly tells of the poet's uneven path in love and of her uneasy relationship to convention:

'Oh need to find a private persona, shape/For life's unease of dictated laws.'

The poet often appears to derive relish from stripping the potentially idyllic of its romantic overcoat and from subverting idealisations of femininity. In 'Absence', she contests the associations of the sonnet in her anti-romantic portrayal of the unfaithful sailor and the frustrated sexuality of the virgin; in 'Tess', she exaggerates the brutality of Alec's supposedly sacrificial murder by exchanging Thomas Hardy's sentimentalised setting for a violated landscape.

'A Dream' is based on one of Vita's vividly remembered dreams. The solitariness which Vita Sackville-West both craved and feared is presented as less than consoling when allied to old age or inescapable routine and surroundings. Again, in 'Spinster', it is the routine which is as restricting as the isolation; the entire loneliness of the woman's life is suggested in the quotidian game of chess; the poem operates at narrative and symbolic levels: the 'leaping knights' are, sadly, only imaginary and the game is merely a temporary substitute for companionship.

Although she lived according to feminist principles of sexual autonomy, and largely rejected heterosexuality, Vita Sackville-West was wary of the label 'feminist'. In *King's Daughter*, *Collected Poems*, and *Solitude* there is some cautious treatment of lesbian subjectivity, but there is always a reticence in the voice of the poems, as there is an intuitive distrust of public discourse in her correspondence. She believed that Virginia Woolf had discovered the flaw to her personality, 'something obscure, that doesn't vibrate . . . something reserved, muted'.[11] In her poetry, Vita knew from experience that she must appear 'dull and rustic' and would not win the approval of the young male writers: 'no doubt Spender, Auden etc. wouldn't call it poetry at all.'[12] In 1932, she used the phrase, 'I am a damned outmoded poet,' which has been held up against her, although it is intended to pay tribute to Enid Bagnold's superior skill.[13] Admittedly, her poetry is more relevant to the beginning than to the end of the decade and yields little when looking for political signs of the times, but many of her poems appeared in collections of modern poetry; one poem was selected for *The Year's Poetry* in 1934,[14] and her poems were often printed in journals ranging from *Time and Tide* and *London Mercury* to the *Poetry Review*. Her poetry books, however, were given scanty reviews in literary papers. In 1950, any remaining confidence was destroyed when she was not selected by the poetry group of the Society of Authors to which she belonged, to read to the Queen, and she stopped writing. She was devastated by this final rejection when she had known outstanding success in the 1920s, her lifelong aspiration was to be a poet and writing poetry made her 'unbearably happy'.[15]

Further Reading

Victoria Glendinning, *Vita: The Life of Vita Sackville-West*, London, Weidenfeld & Nicolson, 1983; Harmondsworth, Penguin, 1984.

Nigel Nicolson, *Portrait of a Marriage*, London, Weidenfeld & Nicolson, 1973; New York, Atheneum, London, Macmillan, 1980.

Nigel Nicolson, ed., *Vita and Harold: The letters of Vita Sackville-West and Harold Nicolson 1910–1962*, London, Weidenfeld & Nicolson, 1992.

Suzanne Rait, *Vita and Virginia: The Work and Friendship of Vita Sackville-West and Virginia Woolf*, Oxford, Oxford University Press, 1993.

Louise de Salvo and Mitchell A. Leaska, eds, *The Letters of Virginia Woolf and Vita Sackville-West*, London, Hutchinson, 1984.

Sissinghurst

THURSDAY. TO V.W.

A tired swimmer in the waves of time
I throw my hands up! let the surface close:
Sink down through centuries to another clime,
And buried find the castle and the rose.
5   Buried in time and sleep,
       So drowsy, overgrown,
That here the moss is green upon the stone,
      And lichen stains the keep.
I've sunk into an image, water-drowned,
10 Where stirs no wind and penetrates no sound,
Illusive, fragile to a touch, remote,
Foundered within the well of years as deep
As in the waters of a stagnant moat.
Yet in and out of these decaying halls
15 I move, and not a ripple, not a quiver,
Shakes the reflection though the waters shiver,
My tread is to the same illusion bound.
Here, tall and damask as a summer flower,
Rise the brick gable and the spring tower;
20   Invading Nature crawls
With ivied fingers over rosy walls,
     Searching the crevices,
Clasping the mullion, riveting the crack
     Binding the fabric crumbling to attack,
25 And questing feelers of the wandering fronds
Grope for interstices,
Holding this myth together under-seas,
     Anachronistic vagabonds!

And here, by birthright far from present fashion,
30 As no disturber of the mirrored trance

I move, and to the world above the waters
 Wave my incognisance.
For here, where days and years have lost their number,
I let a plummet down in lieu of date,
35 And lose myself within a slumber
  Submerged, elate.

For now the apple ripens, now the hop,
And now the clover, now the barley-crop;
Spokes bound upon a wheel forever turning,
40 Wherewith I turn, no present manner learning;
Cry neither "Speed your processes!" nor "Stop!"
I am content to leave the world awry
(Busy with politic perplexity,)
If still the cart-horse at the fall of day
45 Clumps up the lane to stable and to hay,
And tired men go home from the immense
  Labour and Life's expense
That force the harsh recalcitrant waste to yield
Corn and not nettles in the harvest field;
50 This husbandry, this castle, and this I
   Moving within the deeps,
Shall be content within our timeless spell,
Assembled fragments of an age gone by,
While still the sower sows, the reaper reaps,
55 Beneath the snowy mountains of the sky,
And meadows dimple to the village bell.
So plods the stallion up my evening lane
And fills me with a mindless deep repose,
  Wherein I find in chain
60 The castle, and the pasture and the rose.

Beauty, and use, and beauty once again
Link up my scattered heart and shape a scheme
Commensurate with a frustrated dream.
The autumn bonfire smokes across the woods
65 And reddens in the water of the moat;
As red within the water burns the scythe,
And the moon dwindled to her gibbous tithe
  Follows the sunken sun afloat.
Green is the eastern sky and red the west;
70 The hop-kilns huddle under pallid hoods;
The waggon stupid stands with upright shaft,

As daily life accepts the night's arrest.
Night like a deeper sea engulfs the land,
The castle, and the meadows, and the farm;
75 Only the baying watch-dog looks for harm,
And shakes his chain towards the lunar brand.
In the high room where tall the shadows tilt
As candle-flames blow crooked in the draught,
The reddened sunset on the panes was spilt,
80 But now as black as any nomad's tent
The night-time and the night of time have blent
Their darkness, and the waters doubly sleep.
Over my head the years and centuries sweep,
            The years of childhood flown
            The centuries unknown;
I dream; I do not weep.

                                                1930

Out with a Gun

... But who would loose a gun to-night?
The day in silver stillness ends,
And on the lake such peace descends
That swallows in their evening flight
5 Make music on a level wing.

The trees reflected in the lake
Plunge down to depths that meet the sky;
The water rests without a sigh,
Though little moorhens leave their wake,
10 And insects drop a widening ring.

Confident in this hour emerge
The secret lives from brake and bole,
The coot, the leveret, and the vole,
Tranquil to move about the verge
15 Between the water and the wood.

Christ! has the world not pain enough
That I should shatter with a shot
– As one who crept with conscious plot,
Evil, malevolent; and rough, –
20 This innocence of lowlihood?

Two swallows nest within my house;

I wake at dawn to see them come;
And on my floor let fall the crumb
Of harvest for a duffle mouse
25   Who makes my room his private garth.

Squirrel, take half my nuts; and you,
Leveret, share my springing corn;
Vixen, deride the hunting-horn;
Fear but the owl, small pointed shrew;
And, sweet Saint Francis, haunt my hearth.

To Any M.F.H.

Sanctuary should exist on earth;
Some private place, where life may be.
Some private place for death and birth,
For boisterous love and puppy mirth
5   Between the bracken and the tree.

In such a place, a girdled place,
The refuge of the small pursued,
Shall some similitude of grace
Be caught within the fenced embrace,
10   That guards my leafy solitude;

And no white horse or scarlet sleeve
Shall sprinkle down the woodland ride
Where paths between the chestnuts cleave,
And mists the morning stories thieve
15   From men in different mood astride.

In such a place my foxes should
Live free to mate and breed and kill
Within the ambush of my wood,
Scorning the huntsman's hardihood
20   Hallooing on the stranger's hill.

Though warring men must stain the west
Doubly with sunsets barbarous dye,
Leaving the plumes of manhood's crest,
A shameful yet a proud bequest,
25   In trails of blood across the sky,

Within the acres that I rule,
The little patch of peace I vaunt,

Where ways are safe and shadows cool,
Shall come no scarlet-coated fool
To tease my foxes from their haunt.

Sept. 1932

Nostalgia

That day must come, when I shall leave my friends,
My loves, my garden, and the bush of balm
That grows beside my door, for the world's ends:
A Persian valley where I might find calm.

5   And this is no romance; the place is no
Vague lovely Persia of a poet's tale,
But a very valley where some cornfields grow
And peasants beat the harvest with a flail.

I saw it, as I saw the pigeon-towers
10   Streaked white with dung, and goat-kids born in blood;
And saw the early almond spray its flowers
Through breaches in the wall of sun-burnt mud.

Brutality and beauty shared the sun;
Necessity of crops the river-bed;
15   And I without such sunlight am undone,
Without such rivers wilt unharvested.

1932

September 1939

Sick to our souls we dumbly wait
As though some wild disordered star
Broke from its place, and from afar
Rushed downward like a streak of fate.

5   Nothing remains but active faith
And courage of a high despair,
In moments when we grow aware
Of noble death that is not death.

Absence

No lights are burning in the ivory tower
Like a tall lily in the moonlight risen;

No light, to-night, within the ivory prison.
No golden glow behind the blackened panes
5   Like golden anthers in a pallid flower;
The gates are looped, to-night, with hasps and chains.
Only the little virgin coldly smiling
With carven finger raised to carven lip
In secrecy beneath the latticed moon
10   Preserves her secret, keeps her virgin watch
On silvered fields that to the silver heaven
Lie open as the restless summer sea
Crossed by one tall incautious sailing-ship,
Or love to lover generously given.

1931

Tess

Love thou but me; all other realms I'll give thee
Realms of the wind, the starlight, and the rain.
Love the whole natural world, and I'll forgive thee
If thou but love no mortal limbs again.

5   So generous am I, I would not stint thee;
I spread the whole of nature for thy choice
Only, with my own cipher would imprint thee,
That thou should'st answer to my single voice.

Oh then beware! for should'st thou stray or falter
10   From that high mark my arrogance has set,
Stern as a priest I'll stretch thee on an altar
And in revenge all tenderness forget.

Then when the rising sun makes summer shadow,
I'll take a knife and stretch thee on a stone
15   Scooped for the blood to soak a Wiltshire meadow,
When dawn and death shall find us there, alone.

1931

A Dream

Down the long path beneath the garden wall,
She stooped, setting her plants in the winter dusk.
She knew she must make an end of setting her plants,
Though why she must make an end she nothing knew.

5   Was it the end of the year that made her urgent?
Was it the end of the day? for night came down,
And the heavy sky grew black above the wall,
And the trees were quiet in a stillness worse than storm
As the great white stealthy flakes began to fall,
10   But still she stooped with her trowel, setting her plants.

And the ground grew white with the imperceptible drift
Of the silent snow from a black and loaded heaven,
And candles came around her, stuck in silver;
Candelabra of silver, with horns of flame,
15   Burning the snow to a ruddy glow as she set
The fragile year's-end plants of her dying hopes.

But the candles failed to mount with the mounting snow;
The silver bases and then the silver stems
Were buried under the drift, and the drift invaded
20   The very candles and stems of tender wax,
So that the flames alone remained above the snow,
But the flames persisted, travelling as she travelled,
And the snow touched them not, nor melted they the snow.

Then came the fallow deer with delicate steps,
25   Printing their steps around her as she stooped,
And their antlers burned with little flames at tip,
Little daggers of gold at every point,
Pricket and sorel and buck, and the doe with her fawn.
  And she knew that she neared the end of the garden path,
30   And the deer and the buried candles travelled with her,
But still she knew that she would not make an end
Of setting her plants before the shroud came round her.

1931

Spinster

She played her game of chess, alone, when day was done;
So solitary, that she played alone,
Finding no friend to be her adversary.
So she made reckoning against herself,
5   Pondering over black and scarlet checks
So square, so motley in their strange convention,
Bright as the pattern on a herald's tabard,
And stylised as the King and Queen of Spades.

[118]

She cupped her chin in lamplight, as the checks
10   Developed each their own complexity:
Oblation of the sacrificial pawn,
Antics of equine, freakish, leaping knight,
And sly episcopal obliquity;
The rush of reckless queens, the sour retreat
10   Of kings behind a slavish rash defence,
And general scheme with falsely neat relation
To life denied her simple scope of grasp.

1931

Valediction

Do not forget, my dear, that once we loved.
Remember only, free of stain or smutch,
That passion once went naked and ungloved,
And that your skin was startled by my touch.

5   And though the processes of mortal change
Delude you now to different belief,
Consider only that the heart's a strange
Quick turn-coat, undeserving of your grief.

Forget, – regret, should these two words be brothers?
10   If rhyme to rhyme be kith, so let them be!
Pass from my heart towards the heart of others:
But in your passing, half-remember me.

1932

Extract from *Solitude*

Life I do love, and still in pain protest
I grasped it whole with no protective glove;
I loved it with its tigers and its lions;
Not as the thrush that with her mottled breast
5   Scoops for her mottled eggs a cosy nest,
But like a thousand fiery-bound Ixions
Wheeled the extravagant measure of my love.
As cats who run the leopard in their veins
I ran the love of life, sagacious, wild,
10   A freshet from the source, a stumbling child,
An old man near the grave, an ardent boy
Shaking the noisy shackles of his chains,
Yet saw myself for what I was, – a toy.

A toy, a hazard cast upon the air,
15   Informed by some unknown especial sense;
An unexplained, unique coincidence,
Required to suffer more than it could bear,
Yet through the grammar of life's gibberish
Straining the letters of some alphabet
20   To fit my own especial epithet;
Trailing my net to catch the silver fish,
To trap the finch within a knotted net,
The magpie in a snare.
Proud boast! for one who saw the shortened years
25   From womb to tomb in all their chance and dance,
Our laughter yet more piteous than our tears,
Our knowledge than our ignorance.

                            (*pp. 22–3*)

[...]

Thus love, bright charlatan, besieged my heart,
And took my time, and set my sense apart,
Wasting my days and nights, when other streams
Were damned by those fair, wild, delusive dreams
5   We label love, and then as truth impart.

Those cheap and easy loves! but what were they,
Those rash intruders into darkest lairs?
Mere brigands ravishing a secret tract,
Mere sparks in wanton fire
10   Blazing the straw of desiccate desire,
Mere breaths, delusive nothings of a day
To nothing vanished and from little born,
Less than a transient breath across the corn,
A whim that scarcely swerves our selfish way.

15   Like crooked chessman-knight that leaps the squares
Sideways, and takes his foeman unawares
By mathematical design attacked,
We take a heart, and leave our own intact.

                            (*pp. 28–9*)

Notes

1 Letter to Harold, 14 Feb. 1933, Nigel Nicolson, *Vita and Harold*, p. 238.

2 See Victoria Glendinning, Preface, *Vita*.

3 Vita Sackville-West, 31 January 1927, Louise de Salvo, and Mitchell A. Leaska, *Letters*, p. 187.

4 Vita Sackville-West, 3 December 1928, ibid., p. 315.

5 Vita Sackville-West, 24 January 1933, ibid., p. 404.

6 ibid.

7 Review of *Collected Poems*, *New Statesman*, included as an appendix to *Solitude*.

8 Letter to Harold, 1946, Victoria Glendinning, *Vita*, p. 340.

9 Vita Sackville-West, 'All I can say is, rhythm and I are out of gear', letter to Virginia Woolf, 8 April 1926, Louise de Salvo and Mitchell A. Leaska, *Letters*, p. 131.

10 Vita Sackville-West, 16 September 1939, ibid., p. 457.

11 Vita Sackville-West, Letter to Harold, 20 November, 1926, Nigel Nicolson, *Vita and Harold*, p. 173.

12 Vita Sackville-West, Letter to Harold, 13 February 1939, ibid., p. 310.

13 'To Enid Bagnold', *CP*, p. 247.

14 'On the Lake', *The Year's Poetry*, ed. Denys Kilham Roberts *et al.*, London, The Bodley Head, 1934, p. 52.

15 Vita Sackville-West, Letter to Harold, 1946, Victoria Glendinning, *Vita*, p. 340.

15
E.J. Scovell
b. 1907

1944   *Shadows of Chrysanthemums*, London, Routledge
1946   *The Midsummer Meadow*, London, Routledge
1956   *The River Steamer*, London, Cresset
1982   *The Space Between*, London, Secker & Warburg
1986   *Listening to Collared Doves*, Herts, Mandeville
1988   *Collected Poems*, Manchester, Carcanet
1991   *Selected Poems*, Manchester, Carcanet

E.J. (Joy) Scovell was educated at home in South Yorkshire and Buckingham-shire, at Castleton School (the same establishment as the Brontë sisters), and at Somerville College, Oxford. As an undergraduate, she contributed to various university journals – she was one of the few women in *Oxford Poetry* – and edited *Fritillary*, the magazine of the Oxford Women's Colleges. Having graduated in 1930, she took secretarial posts in London, including one with *Time and Tide*, where she worked with the literary editor Ellis Roberts. In 1937, she married Charles Elton and moved back to Oxford; in 1938, they embarked on one of several visits to the Americas as part of her husband's ecological work on tropical rain forests; he died in 1991. She still lives in Oxford and visits her son in Scotland and daughter in the West Indies.

Nearly all the poems in the first two parts of *Collected Poems* were composed in the 1930s. E.J. Scovell started writing poetry in the 1920s and wrote more in the 1930s than at any other time, but she did not initially publish her work, perceiving it to be insufficiently political for the prevailing fashion. She was conscious of the influence of the Audenesque, but did not attempt to connect with modern movements; consequently, she usually received delayed recognition but her poems have never been outmoded either. In addition to her own collections, she has written translations of the Italian poet Giovanni Pascoli. *The River Steamer* and *Selected Poems* were both Poetry Book Society recommendations; she has given poetry readings and taken part in discussions on BBC radio; in 1989 she received a Cholmondeley award and in 1992 a Cheltenham Festival Prize.

Scovell has sometimes been misrepresented as being primarily preoccupied with domesticity, largely because of her 'Poems in Infancy', which were included in Anne Ridler's supplement to the *Faber Book of Modern Verse* in 1951. At the time, they were uncommon in chronicling the first years of a child and in celebrating parenthood. The everyday world depicted is not, however, closeted. The poems are not 'withdrawals from contemporary reality'[1] but a concentration *on* experience. In 'The City Worker', for example, the clipped rhythm reconstructs the routine of the clerk, but does not represent his or the narrator's point of view. Jem Poster points out the spatial element in the descriptions, '[the] depiction of the mundane, the domestic, the familiar, is not the goal, but a point of departure',[2] and Alan Brownjohn circumspectly noted the 'tough talent at work under the surface calm'.[3] Anne Ridler, who helped with the publication of *The River Steamer*, identifies the combination of clarity and undertone as achieved in the minutely observed images and a 'power from our sense of evocation rather than description'.

E.J. Scovell's unique vision which gives away nothing of the seer has sometimes confounded critical assessment. This perspicacity was admired by Geoffrey Grigson, who included eight poems in *Poetry of the Present: An Anthology of the Thirties and After*.[4] He championed her skill in depicting things as they are at the moment of observation and pronounced her 'a poet less concerned with celebrity and self-importance than with being alive and in love ... the purest woman poet of our time'.[5] By 'pure' he accounted the manipulation of language so that it was the unobtrusive lens into the world of objects and events. Since then, her meticulous sketches of people and places have been steadily appreciated, inspiring a revival of interest during the 1980s.

The poems included here were written before the experiences of motherhood, although her sensitive eye for mothers and children is apparent. 'A Stranger' and 'The Poor Mother' exemplify the poet's skill at opening windows on to the world of people. E.J. Scovell believes that the job of the poet is to *observe* - she claims to 'write what I see' – but not to comment, for all that can be known is the moment. This restraint is what Carol Rumens discerns as 'a modern sensibility ... her unemphatic, undeceived and honest observation of *what is*'.[6]

The rhythms are not those of the conversational idiom, although inattentive reading can miss the disquieting ironies. She has an unsentimental sympathy for the dispossessed; the delicacy of a poem like 'Flowers' is nothing to do with flora but with non-conformity; the value of individuality, in the face of mass-productivity, was a common feature in Thirties literature. The snapshots of women frequently capture their social dislocation and consequent psychological disintegration. 'The Suicide', 'The Vain Girl Jilted', 'A Stranger', 'Death from Cancer' and 'The Poor Mother' are all typical of using a single sketch to suggest a wider picture. Significantly, they are pictures of women on their own; suffering is described, but without the pity which would diminish their dignity. There is ambiguity in images such as 'carved' with their simultaneous conjuration of both cruelty and care.

Although she has not found an aesthetic in the feminist movement, E.J. Scovell believes that she never writes from the man's point of view. She is a positive model for younger women poets; her admirers include Anne Stevenson and Carol Rumens, who also attest that the concerns of art should transcend those of gender. Fleur Adcock and Linda France have firmly placed Joy Scovell within their anthologies of this century's women poets.

Further Reading

Charles Brand, ed., *Ten Oxford Poets*, including Anne Ridler and E.J. Scovell, Oxford, Charles Brand, 1978.

Jem Poster, 'In Love with Space', review of *Collected Poems*, *PN Review* 90, vol. 19, no. 4, March /April 1988, pp. 24–7.

Carol Rumens and John Mole, 'A Visionary in Sensible Shoes – The Poetry of E.J. Scovell', *Poetry Review*, 1986, vol. 6, no. 4, pp. 37–40.

Flowers

The first flower grows as high as the sunshine.
The second flower, more deeply planted,
Tilts up its muzzle yet, its serpentine
Light-seeking head, and body slanted.
5   And one curves deeply skirting by a stone,
And one flower rides the air upright.
These all look one way, as if a wind had blown,
And stretch one way, to grasp the light.

And in a dream I saw a flower that bent
10 From earth almost to earth its stem
And did not go the way the others went,
And yet was beautiful like them.

The City Worker

In what I do, I speak.
I place my columns rightly.
Nothing I let unsightly,
Discordant, enter in.
5   So days lie in the week:
Sunday, the white margin.

Formal as church-attending,

Solved as hours of a nun,
From the hour of work begun
10   All the day's hours chime in order
Till the hour of work's ending:
Streets in drained light for a border.

The Suicide

Not daylight and not the dark,
Not even the outdoor evening, ebbing,
Yielded this woman her despair,
Her dead she sought, her drowned and still.
5   Daylight confuses with strong scent.
Darkness is an open door.
Evening is dense with words and tears.

With words we betray the vision.
Words with wind disturb the air,
10   With breath and eye-bright flicker of wings
Between our sight and still despair.
And tears breed pity, pity is
A tune, and music raises comfort,
The old, starved, elastic moon.

15   With her face reared, with her stone bows
She parted left and right through streets
The men like clouds. All things she saw
Her seeing mowed and bound in sheaves.
Yet she was quiet as a mouse
20   Or a small knife that makes its house,
Whose burrow is its own neat size.

And seeing all, she looked beyond
Famished to come to her despair,
And prayed in fear, in rage of will:
25   "Show me sorrow in still air.
For when I say I am betrayed
Wonder or pain confuses me,
Or a star falls and calls my eyes."

In still air, her own room was
30   Like an unlidded consciousness,
No light seen there, but a deep-sea,
Pearl-equal visibility.

In that pool she looked and saw,
Image of truth, the essence sorrow;
In that mirror ran to death.

A Stranger

I saw a woman drag her foot,
Inept pass through the day,
As if she had an idiot child
Who bled her life away;

5   As if her ghost stayed in a room
High under roofs, that none
Could see inside; there nursed a fire
That never must burn down.

There like a piled fire intense
10   Or tree fed by her will,
One lived, unique, a gulf of life
Her life flowed out to fill.

The running children in poor streets
Grazed with their eyes her own.
15   Far in the mountains of her heart
The infertile streams poured down.

Whom all could wound, yet none could touch,
What child or thought or soul,
Terror or pain she tended there
20   Her passing did not tell.

The Poor Mother

"Hush!" she says by rote under the trees
On park seats, with one hand moving the pram.
She holds a child like fate upon her knees
On long train journeys, in the sleepless tram,

5   Like a part of her body, like her heart.
She seems halfnumbed and lost to him, her care,
But her dull touch and words, the kind or tart,
Indifferent, move in his sighing breast like air.

And she waits long with her sick children in

10 Hospital corridors and ante-rooms;
Till the door opens and the rites begin,
Talking with other women low among tombs;

And late goes where deepest his shadow lies
Who is her friend and enemy and lover –
15 Lies over earth and over her and these
The children that he took and carved out of her.

Death from Cancer

Her face, though smaller than a child's, smaller than a flower,
Seemed forged in iron, or seemed quarried from granite,
Or carved in one stroke by lightning entering
The dense heart of a tree.

5 Her body had grown small as suddenly
And strangely as a dream dissolved in morning.
Crying through blankets, it seemed to those who had known her a
woman
Not perished but returned to infancy.

And her skin was delicate and lustreless as woodsorrel,
10 As moths at dusk; but the east and age in its colour;
And not childhood, not lightness, not springing, but all
Close, compact substance was expressed in her.

Gentle and salt in life: black courage
Unwilled as the pain, and losing war without truce
15 Remained for her; for them visions of rock uncovered
By the tides of her comfort going down.

The Vain Girl Jilted

I can take cover
In good men's esteem,
From morning to night.
I can take cover
5 In the grace of being human
From the want of my lover
Who named me a woman.

All day I am clothed
From my head to my feet

10   In common kindness,
In courtesy;

All day my loathed
Flesh covered over
With favour of men –
15   That lost his favour.

At night I am naked.
I weep on my bed.
Night has no voice
But all is said.

Notes

1 Kenneth Allott, ed., *The Penguin Book of Contemporary Verse*, Harmondsworth, Penguin, 1950, p. 211.

2 Jem Poster, 'In Love With Space', p. 24.

3 Alan Brownjohn, 'Collected Lifelines', *Sunday Times*, 20 October 1991, p. 14.

4 Geoffrey Grigson, ed., *Poetry of the Present: An Anthology of the Thirties and After*, London, Phoenix House, 1949.

5 Geoffrey Grigson, see John Mole, *Poetry Review*, p. 37.

6 Carol Rumens, ibid., p. 39.

16
Edith Sitwell
1887–1964

1918 *Clowns' Houses*, Oxford, Blackwell

1920 *The Wooden Pegasus*, Oxford, Blackwell

1923 *Bucolic Comedies*, London, Duckworth

1924 *The Sleeping Beauty*, London, Duckworth

1925 *Troy Park*, London, Duckworth

1927 *Rustic Elegies*, London, Duckworth

1929 *Gold Coast Customs*, London, Duckworth

1930 *Collected Poems*, London, Duckworth

1933 *Five Variations on a Theme*, London, Duckworth

1936 *Selected Poems*, London, Duckworth

1940 *Poems New and Old*, London, Faber

1943 *Street Songs*, London, Macmillan

1944 *Green Song and Other Poems*, London, Macmillan

1945 *The Song of the Cold*, London, Macmillan

1947 *The Shadow of Cain*, London, John Lehmann

1949 *The Canticle of the Rose: Selected Poems 1920–1947*, London, Macmillan

1950 *Façade and Other Poems 1920–1935*, London, Duckworth

1952 *Selected Poems*, Harmondsworth, Penguin

1953 *Gardens and Astronomers: New Poems*, London, Macmillan

1957 *Collected Poems*, London, Macmillan

1962 *The Outcasts*, London, Macmillan

1965 *Selected Poems*, London, Macmillan

1972 *Wheels 1–6: 1916–1921*, (ed.) reprinted Liechtenstein, Kraus Thompson Organisation

1982 *Collected Poems*, reprinted, London, Macmillan

In addition to the formidable publishing history of her poems, Dame Edith Sitwell was a prolific journalist and critic; she wrote a radio play, published a novel, historical and satirical biographies, edited several poetry anthologies and gave poetry readings and lectures on poetry in Britain, France, Italy and the

United States. She was awarded D.Litts from the Universities of Leeds, Durham and Oxford. Her mountain of publications and later accumulation of literary honours can conceal the efforts which preceded her eventual acclaim. She had to work ceaselessly for financial independence and to overcome the persistence of critics who undermined her writing by grouping her with her brothers, and who deflected attention away from her writing by mocking her personal idiosyncrasies. According to Robin Skelton, when surveying the 1930s, 'It seems as if Sitwell-baiting was a necessary ritual'.[1] In stating that 'the Sitwells belong to the history of publicity rather than of poetry',[2] F.R. Leavis was unjustifiably relegating Edith, along with Osbert and Sacheverell, to a place outside of the movements of modern poetry. It *is* true, however, that controversies over the importance of her poetry have been continual. In mapping English verse, John Press notes that 'The divergences over Edith Sitwell are inseparable from the personal, cultural, social and educational principles and prejudices which have inspired them.'[3]

Edith Sitwell's poems have always been available, but critical discussions have tended to concentrate on her reputation as an aristocratic eccentric. She was self-educated and brought up by governesses at the family estate of Renishaw Hall, Derbyshire, but reacted against her privileged heritage and the 'hell' of her childhood; her father found her 'unsatisfactory' for neither being a male nor conforming to traditional models of femininity. She left home for London in 1914 and channelled her furies about the ills of social conventions into revolutionising poetry. She became radically anti-establishment; her collaborative annual anthology *Wheels* (1916–21) was deliberately controversial and consequently influential on the experimentations with poetic forms which were partly a reaction against the idylls of rural England as celebrated in some so-called Georgian Verse.

As a woman cultivating a public persona, Edith Sitwell risked disapproval. She knew, but was not of, the Bloomsbury writers and dug an independent path. She gave regular tea parties at 22, Pembridge Mansions, and later in life held 'Sesame Parties' at her London club. She also spent time in Paris where she gave readings and held her own against such figures as Gertrude Stein. Although she is the most anthologised woman in collections of modern British poetry, the 1930s was a dry season for her. She suffered from ill health and was recovering from thwarted passion for the homosexual painter Pavel Tchelitchew; her mother died in 1937; she was impecunious through trying to support herself and her former governess, Helen Rootham, who was terminally ill and died of bone cancer in 1938. They had shared the flat in Pembridge Mansions for eighteen years and had moved to Paris in 1932. Edith Sitwell reluctantly concentrated on prose because it was more lucrative: her historical portrait, *Victoria of England* (1931), was a best seller; she wrote a study of Bath, worked on *The English Eccentrics* (1933) and her novel, *I Live Under a Black Sun*, which was published in 1937.

Throughout the 1930s, Edith Sitwell's only poems were 'Romance' and 'Prelude', 'in which I was finding my way'.[4] Nevertheless, she continued to impact on the poetry of the decade: her poems were printed in magazines; a limited illustrated edition of her poem 'Spring' was published; 'Façade' was performed as a ballet; *Collected Poems* was published in 1930, and *Selected Poems* in 1936; she was awarded the Royal Society of Literature's medal for poetry in 1934 and featured prominently in reviews and discussions of Modern Poetry, including Yeats' National Lecture (1936); six of her poems were included in his *The Oxford Book of Modern Verse* (1936). The second and third volumes of her surveys *Pleasures of Poetry* were published in 1931 and 1933. In *Aspects of Modern Poetry*, (1934) she denounced the absolutism of the New Critics, Leavis, Grigson and Wyndham Lewis, and provoked much response in the literary journals, including Grigson's triumphalistic lambastes in *New Verse*.[5] She also had supporters of her arguments and in the 1940s had regained more consistent esteem. For example, she achieved mutual respect with Dylan Thomas, Stephen Spender and Louis MacNeice, whose 'Aubade', at least, has been considered to have been influenced by her experiments.[6] She was later reconciled to Auden and Grigson and her success was at its height in the 1950s.

There is evidence that whilst not writing poems, Edith Sitwell was responding to the new currents as well as reviewing her own style. She had been working on 'Romance' for eighteen months, before its publication in *Five Variations on a Theme*. It is an attempt to salvage 'something eternal from the wreckage of love'.[7] 'Prelude' was printed in *The Year's Poetry*, 1935. The poem is most remarkable for its rhythmic versatility and acoustic clarity. It is typical of the poet's preoccupation with sound: in phrases like 'my plant-shrill blood', Edith Sitwell is unashamed in putting technical effects above sense. Her interest was in texture, even if the symbols did not operate satisfactorily. She characteristically interweaves recurring signifiers of primal forms, such as bones, suns, birds and beasts, with the human soul. Too often, the orchestration is overworked. She is best when straightforward, as in the plain speaking finale of the poem. The closing lines reappear almost identically in her novel and in the poem 'An Old Woman' (1942): the expression of a faith in a unifying life-force of light and growth was an increasingly important antidote to her developing nightmare vision of the world. These poems mark the transition which began with *Gold Coast Customs* in 1929, from the poet as the child's eye to the poet as seer and prophet; she became engrossed by the immutability of death and the 'immense design of the world'. Kenneth Clark identified the fundamental changes in her later poetry, as perceived in 'Prelude', as the move away from littleness and decoration to an 'ampler style, a rhythm capable of sustaining simple, passionate and prophetic statements of belief'.[8] The longer line is one obvious mark of this new direction. Still primarily experimenting with sound, Edith Sitwell's work definitely changed and the poetry of the Second World War restored her reputation as a pioneer. One of the best critical discussions is her own: 'Some Notes on My Own Poetry', which introduce *Collected Poems* and which originally appeared in the *London Mercury*, March 1935.

Edith Sitwell admired Christina Rossetti, but deplored most women's poetry for being undisciplined and over-emotional. She did not brook rivals, but did give credit where she could; she wrote a favourable review of Charlotte Mew's poems[9] and defended Lilian Bowes Lyon. Initially, she believed that women were different – 'Women poets will do best if they realise that male technique is not suitable for them'[10] – but later was more anxious to eliminate the ghettoising of 'women poets' – 'If one can't write like a man, one has no business to write at all.'[11]

Further Reading

Victoria Glendinning, *Edith Sitwell: A Unicorn Among Lions*, London, Weidenfeld & Nicolson, 1981.

John Lehmann and Derek Parker, eds, *Edith Sitwell: Selected Letters*, London, Macmillan, 1970.

Elizabeth Salter, *The Last Years of a Rebel*, London, Michael Joseph, 1967.

Elizabeth Salter and Allanah Harper, eds, *Edith Sitwell: Fire of the Mind, An Anthology*, London, Michael Joseph, (1956) 1976.

Edith Sitwell, *Taken Care Of*, autobiography, London, Hutchinson, 1965.

Extract from *Romance*

FOR RÉE GORER

She grew within his heart as the flushed rose
In the green heat of the long summer grows
Deep in the sorrowful heaven of her leaves.
And this song only is the sound that grieves
5   When the gold-fingered wind from the green veins
Of the rich rose deflowers her amber blood,
The sharp green rains.
Such is the song, grown from a sleepy head,
Of lovers in a country paradise, –
10   You shall not find it where a song-bird flies,
Nor from the sound that in a bird-throat grieves;
Its chart lies not in maps or strawberry leaves.

Green were the pomp and pleasure of the shade

Wherein they dwelt; like country temples green
15 The huge leaves bear a dark-mosaic'd sheen
Like gold on forest temples richly laid.

In that smooth darkness, the gourds dark as caves
Hold thick gold honey for their fountain waves,

Figs, dark and wrinkled as Silenus, hold
20 Rubies and garnets, and the melons cold
Waves dancing.

When the day first gleaned the sun's corn-sheaves
They walked among those temples of the leaves;
And the rich heat had made them black as cloud
25 Or smooth-leaved trees; they lay by waters loud,
And gold-stringed citherns of loud waters made
A madrigal, a country serenade.

But Time drifts by as the long-plumaged lands
And the dark swans whose plumes seem weeping leaves
30 In the shade's richest splendour, – these drift by.
And sometimes he would turn to her and sigh:

'The bright swans leave the wave . . . so leave not me,
With Æthiopaea, smooth Aërope:
Amid the pomp and splendour of the shade
35 Their rich and leafy plumes a lulling music made.

Dark are their plumes, and dark the airs that grew
Amid those weeping leaves.
Plantations of the East drop precious dew
That, ripened by the light, rich leaves perspire,
40 Such are the drops that from the bright swans' feathers flew.

Come then, my pomp and pleasure of the shade,
Most lovely cloud that the hot sun made black
As dark-leaved swans.

Come then, O precious cloud,
45 Lean to my heart. No shade of some rich tree
Shall pour such splendour as your heart to me.'

So these two lovers dreamed the time away
Beside smooth waters like the honey waves
In the ripe melons that are dark as caves;
50 Eternity seemed but a summer day.

And they forgot, seeing the Asian train
Of waves upon the glittering wide sea main
And rich gold waves from fountain caverns run,
That all the splendour of the eastern sun,
55 And many a rose-shaped heart, must lie beneath
The maps on strawberry leaves dark green as snows,
With amber dust that was a nymph or rose –

And worlds more vast lie ruined by sad Time
That is the conqueror of our green clime.
60 For even the beasts eschew the shrunken heart
That dieth of itself, small deaths devour –
Or that worm mightier than death's – the small
corroding hour.

[...]

So winter fell; the heart shaped like the rose
Beneath the mountain of oblivion lies
65 With all death's nations and the centuries.
And this song ending fades like the shrill snows,

Dim as the languid moon's vast fading light
That scatters sparkles faint and dim and chill
Upon the wide leaves round my window-sill
70 Like Æthiopaea ever jewelled bright ...

So fading from the branches the snow sang
With a strange perfume, a melodious twang
As if a rose should change into a ghost –
A ghost turn to a perfume on the leaves.

NOTE: For a later variation of the song, and certain lines in 'Metamorphosis', see 'Most Lovely Shade', *CP*, 1982, p. 321.

Prelude

FOR GEOFFREY GORER

When our long sun into the dark had set
And made but winter branches of his rays –
I left my heart.
So doth a shadow leave
5 The body when our long dark sun is gone.

Now the black chaos of the Polar night
Melts in the hearts of the forgotten Dead –
The tears turned ice about each loveless head
Are changed into bird-plumaged bird-voiced springs
10 And the sap rises like a bird that sings.

The cold wind creaking in my plant-shrill blood
Seems spring beginning in some earthen bud
Though immemorial, the winter's shade
Furred my cold blood wherein plant, beast, are laid
15 In that dark earth from which shall spring the soul

As dark and broken hints of sciences
Forgotten, and strange satyrine alliances
Of beast and soul lie hidden in the old
Immensity and desert of the cold.

20 Hoarse as a dog's bark the furled heavy leaves
Are hairy as a dog: furred fire barks for the shape
Of hoarse-voiced animals; cold air agape
Whines to be shut in the water's shapes and plumes;
All things break from the imprisoning winter's glooms.

25 All things, all hearts awake –
Until the gold within the miser's heart
Would buy the siren isles and many a chart
From dream to dream, and the death-blinded eyes
See beyond wild bird-winged discoveries.

30 All creatures praise the sun in their degrees:
The mother bear with thick forestial fur
And grumbling footsteps, lumbering primal sleep
Of the winter earth, as furry as a bear
And grumbling deep,
35 No longer sees her cubs as a black blot
As clots of thick black darkness; primal form
shaped from that thick night –
Begins from this black chaos: life is light.

The stunted long-armed gardener mossed as trees
40 Has known before his birth –
For he was born and shaped close to the earth –
Best of all things are water, and hot gold
Of the rough fruitful sun: best of all things are these.
So the slow gold of his hot days and rays

45 Ripened within our earth and changed to fruits,
   So the cold twisted water changed to roots
   Of apple-trees.

   But I, a harpy like a nightingale,
   A nightingale that seems a harpy, mourn
50 With my heart changed now from a black blind stone
   That rolls down the abyss, to a ghost gone
   Or a black shadow cast
   Upon the dust where gossips of mean Death
   The small and gilded scholars of the Fly
55 That feed upon the crowds and their dead breath
   Still buzz and stink where the bright heroes die
   Of the dust's rumours and the old world's fevers
   Sometimes in the arena like a drum
   My heart sounds, calls the heroes from their shade
60 Till with the march of tides, those tall ghosts come
   Where Fortune, Virtue, Folly, Wisdom, these –
   Mimes garbed as aeons, by horizons bound, –
   With monstrous trumpetings of suns at war
   Amid earth-quaking rumour of crowds whispering
65 And bull-voiced bellowings of tropic light
   Contend . . .
   Upon the upturned faces of the blind,
   The crooked has a shadow light makes straight,
   The shallow places gain their depth again,
70 It comes to bless;
   And man-made chasms between man and man
   Of creeds and tongues are filled.
           The guiltless light
   Remakes all things and men in holiness.

Notes

1 Robin Skelton, *Poetry of the Thirties*, Harmondsworth, Penguin, 1964, p. 29.
2 F.R. Leavis, *New Bearings in Modern Poetry*, London, Chatto & Windus, 1932, p. 73.
3 John Press, *A Map of English Verse*, Oxford, Oxford University Press, 1969, p. 157.
4 'Some Notes on My Own Poetry', *Collected Poems*, 1957, p. xii.
5 Geoffrey Grigson, 'New Books on Poetry and Miss Sitwell', *New Verse*, no. 12, December 1934, pp. 13–16.
6 'Mr MacNeice and Miss Sitwell', *Poetry* 63, October. 1943–March 1944, pp. 218–22.

7 Victoria Glendinning, *Edith Sitwell*, p. 181.

8 Kenneth Clark, 'On the Development of Miss Sitwell's Later Style', *Horizon*, July 1947, pp. 7–17.

9 Review of Charlotte Mew, *The Farmer's Bride* and *The Rambling Sailor*, in *The Criterion*, vol. ix. no. 34, October 1929, pp. 130–4.

10 'Some Observations on Women's Poetry', *Vogue* 1925; Elizabeth Salter and Allanah Harper, eds, *Fire of the Mind*, p. 189.

11 Letter to Lincoln Kirstein, May 1950, Victoria Glendinning, *Edith Sitwell*, p. 164.

17
Stevie Smith
1902–1971

1937 *A Good Time Was Had By All*, London, Cape
1938 *Tender Only to One*, London, Cape
1942 *Mother, What is Man?*, London, Cape
1950 *Harold's Leap*, London, Cape
1957 *Not Waving but Drowning*, London, Cape
1958 *Some are More Human than Others: A Sketch-book*, London, Gabberbocchus
1962 *Selected Poems*, London, Longmans
1966 *The Frog Prince*, London, Longmans
1971 *Two in One*, London, Longmans
1972 *Scorpion and Other Poems*, London, Longmans
1975 *Collected Poems*, London, Allen Lane
1978 *Selected Poems*, Harmondsworth, Penguin
1981 *Me Again: The Uncollected Writings Of Stevie Smith*, London, Virago
1983 *Stevie Smith: A Selection*, ed. Hermione Lee, London, Faber

Born in Hull, Florence Margaret Smith lived in London from the age of three. At Palmers Green High School, she considered herself to be rather 'mal vue' and then found the environment of the prestigious North Collegiate School for Girls repressive, until her final year. She rejected advice to continue with higher education because she did not want to end up teaching, the only career that seemed to be available to women. She continued to be self-educated through her avid and eclectic reading of literature, theology, the classics, art and history. Her notebooks 1924–1930 record her observations from books and of the people she saw on her daily round, both of which became the material for her writing. From 1922, she was employed as Secretary to the publishers Sir George Newnes and Sir Neville Pearson for 30 years. In the posthumous *Me Again*, 18 out of the 60 uncollected poems were written during the 1930s. She wrote prolifically but encountered rejection after rejection from publishers. In 1935, one publisher suggested that she try a novel rather than poetry, which she did. In *Novel on Yellow Wallpaper* (1936) it is apparent that she had not been indifferent to discouragement:

what about swelling the mass of cruelty in the world by uncalled for remarks about people's poems, eh? ... You certainly want to think before you go making remarks about people's poems ... you've got my poems all wrong.[1]

A breakthrough came after 1935 when her poems were printed in the *New Statesman and Nation* and brought sufficient attention to ensure further publication of individual poems and eventually the first volume in 1937.

Stevie Smith went on to publish many more volumes and has been widely anthologised, although the narrow range of the poems chosen can misrepresent the enormity of her output. Her life has been better chronicled than her work. Frances Spalding's excellent critical biography illuminates both the work and the poet together, and helps to contest some of the personal myths surrounding Stevie Smith. She is too often famed as the rather idiosyncratic spinster who nursed her aunt 'Lion' and who engaged wholly with life, but seemed to prefer death. In her later years, she was renowned for her live performances where she sang her poems and matched her theatrical manner to the dramatic conversation pieces of her poems. Jeni Couzyn identifies Stevie Smith's magic as 'a kind of dare-devil dance with poetic forms'.[2] It is true that the delights in reversal sometimes correspond to the dimensions of the musical score, but the cleverness of the syntactical complexities, rather than their effects, is rarely acknowledged. Although Stevie Smith achieved national recognition through winning the Queen's Gold Medal for poetry in 1969, critical reception has rarely been unequivocal. From the outset, the obvious individuality of the poems has aroused both admiration – Sylvia Plath was a self-professed 'addict' – and scepticism.

One reason for the scarcity of serious analysis of her poetry, is that it has been found to be unclassifiable. The unclassifiability of the poetry, however, is its achievement: it deliberately disarms ready-made responses in order to question the ready-made responses themselves. Analysis of the poetry seldom goes beyond observation of her originality or her notorious 'off-key conversational sing-song'.[3] Although references to Stevie Smith usually mention her voice, Seamus Heaney is unusual in attempting to define it: 'It is the whole question of the relationship between a speaking voice, a literary voice (or style) and a style of speech shared by and typical of a certain social grouping.'[4]

At a time when the radio was concerned to nationalise BBC received pronunciation, the undertones of the educated English, which Seamus Heaney identified, are implicitly mocked through mimicry, or contrast; at the same time, there is recognition of the confidence and power which they exude. In 'A Portrait', for example, the capital letters of Education, Edifying and Unusual, inflate the status of intellectual debate, whilst the exaggeration of upper class accent deflates it when it is pretence or pretentiousness. In the complementary poem 'Portrait', the tones imitate the affectation of the literary critic whose self-appointed superiority is frequently undermined throughout her writing: 'they killed a poet by neglect' ('They Killed'),[5] or,

> There was an old poet lay dying
> And as he lay dying, said he, (said he)
> I've done much better as a literrury editor
> Than a writing of poetry
>
> ('The Old Poet')[6]

The mixture of limerick, lyric and misspelt prose is perhaps what explains Philip Larkin's dismissal of the poems as 'facetious bosch'.[7] Disregard for convention is, however, a contrived and political gesture. By integrating folk culture, ballads, nursery rhymes, hymn tunes, and proverbial sayings, which belong to all age and social groups, with traditionally esteemed and established referents, class distinctions are rendered irrelevant. The brevity of 'Sigh No More' is one of the strategies which expose the vacuity and deception of rhetoric itself: the first line – 'Sigh no more ladies and gentleman at all' – evokes the sequitur, 'men are deceivers all' and the title of the play from which it is taken – *Much Ado About Nothing*. When displaced, the refrain of love contrasts the mythical world of romantic love or of Elizabethan Merrie England to the self-destruction of modern technology: the sweet song of the speaker is revealed as a sugared pill in the cryptic prose of the final sentence, 'another hundred years you won't be here'.

In many ways, Stevie Smith was ahead of her time: the irreverence of her literary referentiality, the indiscernible shifts between parody and pastiche and the disregard for conventional distinctions between disciplines or cultures, smack of postmodern practice. As Martin Pumphrey points out, Stevie Smith's poetry is 'metacommunication': the question it provokes is whether it is play or serious, and having to ask the question is itself the substance of the poem.[8] She does not, therefore, merely retreat into playful aesthetics. Even though a poem like 'Via Media Via Dolorosa' suggests the almost Christlike agony of the omniscient or liberal mind, the representation of both sides is a political act in assessing the status quo. Her socialist sympathies are evident in her disturbing of traditions and in giving a voice to those without – children, women, and the socially disadvantaged. Her political sensibilities are recorded in her prose, such as 'more talkie from Naomi Mitchison, and she's got world problems on the brain too.'[9] Stevie Smith's response to world problems or to increasing mass production was to challenge mindless conformity and attack 'groupismus'.[10] State control and organised religion were to be feared for being over tidy. Individuality is again and again the message and medium of the sketch poems. Her opposition to institutionalised uniformity, her intolerance of social injustice and her sensitivity to the ill-treatment of artists make her clearly of her epoch and put her firmly within the conventional boundaries of Thirties poets.

The dialectic of mass culture versus cultural elitism is dramatised in 'Sterilization' and 'Salon d'Automne'. Highbrow pontificating is typically mingled with the popular idiom so that it is impossible to detect a privileging of either; consequently there appears to be equal suspicion of both specialisation and mediocrity:

> And soon all our minds will be flat as a pancake
> With no room for genius, exaltation or heartache

In a later poem, 'The Suburban Classes', Stevie Smith typically resists patronising the masses: instead it is the dismissive distance of the superior voice which is at fault:

> There is far too much of the suburban classes
> Spiritually not geographically speaking. They're asses.
> Menacing the greatness of our beloved England they lie,
> Propogating their kind in an eight-roomed stye.[11]

Evidently cognisant of the debates about tradition and the individual talent, neither the speaker nor the poet can be dismissed as naïve.

Stevie Smith's poetry may be Audenesque in aiming for a community of shared assumptions between the poet and the audience and in positioning the speaker on the same rung as the listeners. It is not light-hearted verse, however; the unease or 'funny feelings' are caused by her unrelenting psychological realism which is craftily effected in devices such as the child's voice in 'Landrecie' or the candid epigrams of 'Two Friends' and 'Revenge'. These poems demonstrate Stevie Smith's tendency to represent individual rather than universal evil; similarly, she depicts individual oppression in order to expose institutional wrongs.

Stevie Smith's feminism, as her socialism, is in her portraits of powerlessness. Betrayal is a common situation, especially of girlfriends and wives, regardless of social status. There are assertive women of the moneyed classes, like the mother-in-law in 'Octopus', but women are more often the casualties of man's freedom to choose. 'Marriage I Think' is the retrospection of the abandoned wife who was punished for daring to speak her mind and in 'The Word', Sally Soo is vainly waiting for the fulfilment of empty promises. In 'The Ballet of the Twelve Dancing Princesses', Stevie Smith questions the attraction and elusiveness of aesthetic perfection. Ultimately, Stevie Smith's textual politics are in her rejections of stereotype and her disregard for the discourses of power, whether of bureaucracy, royalty, aristocracy or academia: by disrupting familiar syntactical or formal structures, she challenges their associated assumptions and cultural authority. Consequently, the authority of her writing derives from this persistent transgression of conventional frontiers: in overturning preconceptions, the hidden corners of the individual or national unconscious are exposed.

It is tempting to seek security in searching for the persona of the poet or in dismissing the poems as odd or strange. Even Heaney, as many others, eventually flounders and decides on the word 'eccentric' for the poems. It is tantalising, but impossible, to detect the authentic voice of the poet: she is all and none of the metrically constructed voices:

> You will say: But your poems are all story poems, you keep yourself hidden. Yes. But all the same, my whole life is in these poems ... everything I have lived through, and done, and seen, and read and imagined and thought and argued. Then why do I turn them all upon other people, imaginary people, the people I create? It is because ... it gives proportion and eases the pressure.[12]

Further Reading

Jack Barbera and William McBrien, eds, *Stevie: A Biography of Stevie Smith*, London, Heinemann, 1985.

Seamus Heaney, 'A Memorable Voice' [1976], *Preoccupations: Selected Prose 1968–1978*, London, Faber, 1980, pp. 199–201.

Martin Pumphrey, 'Play, fantasy and strange laughter: Stevie Smith's uncomfortable poetry', *Critical Quarterly*, vol. 28, no. 3, Autumn 1986, pp. 85–96.

Frances Spalding, *Stevie Smith: A Critical Biography*, London, Faber, 1988.

A Portrait

I never know what to say
When I'm in company,
I feel quite tonguetied and shy,
I'm a perfect misery.
5   It really is tantalising,
And after the Education I've had
Surprising.
There's nothing I'd rather say
Than something Edifying and Unusual.

9.12.37

Portrait

Mr. Petty-Pie
Keeps his masterpieces in his head,
He is a better tactician than I.

Silent, silent thought.
5   Never to be brought
To the printed page,

Weave a subtle shade.
O'er the facey-fie
Of little Petty-Pie;
10   And may its lineaments continue to suggest
A wisdom too profound to be expressed

Christmas 1937

Via Media Via Dolorosa

There's so much to be said on either side,
I'll be dumb.
There's so much to be said on either side,
I'll hold my tongue.
5   For years and years I never said a word,
Now I have lost the art: my voice is never heard,
For my apprehension
Snaps beneath the tension
Of what is to be said on either side.

19.8.37

Sterilization

Carve delinquency away,
Said the great Professor Clay.

A surgical operation is just the thing
To make everybody as happy as a king.

5   But the great Dostoievsky the Epileptic
Turned on his side and looked rather sceptic.

And the homosexual Mr. Wilde
Sat in the sunshine and smiled and smiled.

And a similarly inclined older ghost in a ruff
10   Stopped reading his sonnets aloud and said 'Stuff!'

And the certainly eccentric Swift, Crashawe and Donne,
Silently shook hands and thanked God they had gone.

But the egregious Professor Clay
Called on Theopompous and won the day.

15   And soon all our minds will be flat as a pancake,
With no room for genius exaltation or heartache.

And our children and theirs will preen, smirk and chatter,
With not even the sense to ask what is the matter.

21.10.1937

Sigh No More

Sigh no more ladies nor gentlemen at all,
Whatever fate attend or woe befall;
Sigh no more, shed no bitter tear,
Another hundred years you won't be here.

9.9.1937

Salon d'Automne

One thousand and one naked ladies
With a *naiveté*
At once pedantic and unsympathetic
Deck the walls
5   Of the Salon d'Automne.
This is the Slap school of art,
It would be nice
To smack them
Slap, slap, slap,
10 That would be nice.
It is possible
One might tire of smacking them
In time
But not so soon
15 As one tires of seeing them.
We too
Have our pedantic and unsympathetic
School,
It used to show
20 A feeling for animals.
The English are splendid with animals,
There was The Stag at Bay
And Faithful unto Death,
And Man's Best Friend the horse this time
25 Usually under gunfire,
The English are splendid with animals.
That older school

Was perhaps
On an intellectual level
30   With the Salon d'Automne.
Nowadays, of course,
We are more advanced:
The bad modern painter
Has lost the *naiveté*
35   Of that earlier school
And in its place
Has developed a talent
For making the work of his betters
Seem stale
40   By uninspired
Imitation.
Really
This is more tiring
Than the thousand and one
Naked ladies.

1937

The Ballet of the Twelve Dancing Princesses

HAYES COURT, JUNE 1939

The schoolgirls dance on the cold grass
The ballet of the twelve dancing princesses
And the shadows pass

Over their cold feet

5   Above in the cold summer sky the clouds mass
The icy wind blows across the laurel bushes
The sky is hard blue and gray where a cloud rushes
The sky is icy blue it is like the night blue where a star pushes.

But it is not night
10   It is daytime on an English lawn.
The scholars dance. The weather is as fresh as dawn.
Dawn and night are the webs of this summer's day
Dawn and night the tempo of the children's play.

Who taught the scholars? Who informed the dance?
15   Who taught them so innocent to advance
So far in a peculiar study? They seem to be in a trance.

[145]

It is a trance in which the cold innocent feet pass
To and fro in a hinted meaning over the grass
The meaning is not more ominous and frivolous than the clouds
    that mass.

20   There is nothing to my thought more beautiful at this moment
Than a vision of innocence that is bound to do something
    equivocal
I sense something equivocal beneath the veneer of an innocent
    spent
Tale and in the trumpet sound of the icy storm overhead there is
    evocable
The advance of innocence against a mutation that is irrevocable
Only in the imagination of that issue joined for a split second is
    the idea beautiful.

Landrecie

What shall I say to the gentlemen, mother,
They stand in the doorway to hear what is said,
Waiting and watching and listening and laughing,
Is there no word that will send them away?

5   What shall I say to the gentlemen, mother,
What shall I say to them, must I say nothing?
If I say nothing, then will they not harm us,
Will they not harm us and shall we not suffer?

What shall I say to the gentlemen, mother?
10   See, they are waiting, and will not depart.
Closed are your eyelids, your lips closed in silence
Cannot instruct me, oh what shall I answer?

December 1937

Revenge

Revenge, Timotheus cries, and in that shout
There's all there is about it and about
Between this man and me, whate'er befall
There is no word more to be said at all.

December 1937

Two Friends

I only asked my friends to be friendly and polite,
I found them indifferent and censorious;
The one I left to silence, the other to reproach:
God send me over all such friends victorious.

Christmas 1937

The Word

Oh where is the word
Said sweet Sally Soo
Oh! where is the word I seek
It cannot be true
5   There is no word from you
To put in my velvet cheek
But the echoes ran
And the silence came
And alone in the cold
10   She is much the same
Oh! where is the word oh! where is it pray
Don't keep me waiting all night and day.

November 1937

Marriage I Think

Marriage I think
For women
Is the best of opiates.
It kills the thoughts
5   That think about the thoughts,
It is the best of opiates.
So said Maria.
But too long in solitude she'd dwelt,
And too long her thoughts had felt
10   Their strength. So when the man drew near,
Out popped her thoughts and covered him with fear.
Poor Maria!
Better that she had kept her thoughts on a chain,
For now she's alone again and all in pain;
15   She sighs for the man that went and the thoughts that stay
To trouble her dreams by night and her dreams by day.

[handwritten note: too intelligent for men to find her attractive]

[147]

The Octopus

Darling little Tom and Harry,
When time comes for you to marry,
Lullaby,
Mother will be close at hand,
5   Close at hand

Little girlies, you who marry
Darling Tom and darling Harry
By and by,
Understand
10   Mother will be close at hand,
Close at hand

Christmas 1937

Notes

1 Stevie Smith, *Novel on Yellow Wallpaper*, (London, Cape, 1936) London, Virago, 1980, p. 149.
2 Jeni Couzyn, ed., *The Bloodaxe Book of Contemporary Women Poets*, Newcastle upon Tyne, Bloodaxe Books, 1985, p. 37.
3 Fleur Adcock, *The Faber Book of 20th Century Women's Poetry*, London, Faber, 1987, p. 14.
4 Seamus Heaney, 'A Memorable Voice', *Preoccupations*, p. 200.
5 Stevie Smith, *Me Again*, 1981, p. 227.
6 Stevie Smith, *Me Again*, p. 225.
7 Philip Larkin, 'Stevie Goodbye', *Observer*, 23 January 1972, p. 28.
8 Martin Pumphrey, *Critical Quarterly*, p. 95.
9 Stevie Smith, *Me Again*, p. 259.
10 Stevie Smith, *Over the Frontier*, (London, Cape, 1938) London, Virago, 1980, p. 136.
11 'The Suburban Classes', *SP*, 1978, p. 27.
12 Stevie Smith, Radio Talk, 15 June 1966, in Frances Spalding, *Stevie Smith*, p. 198.

18
Sylvia Townsend Warner
1893–1978

1925 *The Espalier*, London, Chatto & Windus
1928 *Time Importuned*, London, Chatto & Windus
1931 *Opus 7*, London, Chatto & Windus
1932 *Rainbow*, New York, Alfred Knopf
1933 *Whether a Dove or a Seagull*, with Valentine Ackland, New York, Viking; London, Chatto & Windus, 1934
1960 *Boxwood*, London, Chatto & Windus
1968 *King Duffus and Other Poems*, London and Wells, Clare, Son & Co. Ltd
1980 *Twelve Poems*, London, Chatto & Windus
1982 *Collected Poems*, Manchester, Carcanet
1985 *Selected Poems*, Manchester, Carcanet

Sylvia Townsend Warner was the daughter of a housemaster at Harrow School where she was educated privately and at home. She studied music and became a distinguished musicologist in London. From 1917 to 1927 she worked as an editor on the ten volume *Tudor Church Music* which was sponsored by the Carnegie Trust and published by Oxford University Press. She had a lengthy affair with a male colleague before her quasi-marriage to Valentine Ackland in 1932. She was used to solitude, kept a private journal and was a prolific correspondent, but was also something of a public figure through her left-wing allegiances. Her political commitment, which has been underestimated in biographical and literary criticism, brought her in touch with many like-minded writers including Nancy Cunard and Naomi Mitchison. During the First World War she worked in a munitions factory, and during the Second World War developed a talent for public speaking through giving lectures on pacifist and socialist initiatives. She published ten volumes of short stories, nine books of poetry, seven novels, a biography of T.H. White, a translation of Proust's *Contre Sainte-Beuve* and several essays and reviews. She was encouraged in her writing by the editors of Chatto & Windus and by David Garnett. In the United States she was more of a celebrity where her popularity was established by Louis Untermeyer. He drew attention to her poems in the *New Yorker* in May 1936.

Although she intended her poems to be as significant as her prose, she is best known for her short story writing while her reputation as a poet has been mostly posthumous. Many of the previously uncollected poems in *Collected Poems* were composed during the 1930s.

Sylvia Townsend Warner's partnership with Valentine Ackland began in 1930. They spent 16 months in a manor house in Norfolk, but otherwise, during the 1930s, they were based in Dorset, first at West Chaldon and then in a bigger house in Frome Vauchurch. After 1933 they became tireless in their activities connected with the British Communist Party and with writers who were concerned about cultural freedom; she joined the Left Book Club and became an executive committee member of the Association of Writers for Intellectual Liberty. In 1936, she went as a British delegate to the International Peace Congress in Brussels, organised by the Communist Party, and in 1937 to the Congress of the International Association in Defence of Culture in Madrid and Valencia. The association aimed for an international exchange of literature and to fight against war, fascism and 'everything that menaces culture'.[1] At home, she was a founder member of the local Readers and Writers Group which was affiliated to the Left Book Club and she was also secretary to the Dorset Peace Council. During the Spanish Civil War she, with Valentine, joined the Red Cross volunteers in Spain and 'wrote as much as anybody did about the war'.[2] Her letters and notebooks are evidence of her admiration for the determination and spirit of the people of Barcelona and her anti-fascist articles were published in *Time and Tide* and *Left Review*.

The poems based on her two visits to Spain have mostly been 'ignored and ... disguised by critical fashion'[3] although two were included in *Poems from Spain* (1939), edited by Stephen Spender. Like W.H. Auden, Sylvia Townsend Warner could write poetry of 'reporting journalism'. 'El Heroe', about the death of the unknown soldier, is a discreet snapshot, having the 'paradoxical union of subtlety and simplicity' admired by Louis Untermeyer,[4] whereas 'Port Bou' has the immediacy of an eye-witness account and 'Journey to Barcelona' a more didactic note. 'Waiting at Cerbere', 'Benicasim',[5] her translations of Spanish poems and two prose extracts are included in *The Penguin Book of Spanish Civil War Verse*. Two other uncollected poems on Spain, 'Red Front' and 'In This Midwinter' – both were printed in *Left Review* in 1935[6] – are discussed at length by Barbara Brothers who attributes Sylvia Townsend Warner's 'exile from literary history' to the apparent paradox of her radical spirit and her formal poeticism;[7] in addition, her gender explains why her politics have not been taken seriously by the makers of poetic canons.[8]

Sylvia Townsend Warner clearly should have belonged to the canonised poetry of the Thirties. Her commitment to the cause of the Spanish Republicans was an extension of her opposition to the injustices of class inequality; she had, 'a resolute understanding and intolerance of social conditions ... the racially ineligible, the economically disinclined and the others consigned to rap at the back door of the castle are Warner's subjects'.[9] In her poems, as in her prose, Warner attacks institutions and bureaucracies which perpetuate poverty and illiteracy. 'Opus 7', for example, is a twelve page mock-epic which dramatises the exploitation of the poor. In the poet's words, it is a 'truthful pastoral in the jog-trot English couplet ... about a comfortless old woman in a village who turned a random flower-patch into a commercial success in order to buy drink to warm her old bones'.[10] As a communist with a concern for the plight of the rural poor, Sylvia Townsend Warner was writing out of 'the discovery that the pen could be used as a sword'.[11]

'Song for a Street-Song' illustrates how the dramatic quality of the poems also derives from the structural ironies where popular forms and candid statements are incorporated with cultivated registers and poetic diction. It uses the street song as an emblem of community life which is threatened by national upheavals; the 'rat-a-plan' is at once the innocent play of children, the scheming of politicians and the approaching drumbeat of war. The changing relative pronouns incorporate several perspectives whilst the blunt commentary interrupts the song:

> And flesh that lay beside you in the marriage bed
> mangles your own heart when it is ripped to shreds

> And freedom in muck and warfare maimed and defiled
> Is a bitterer hazard than loss of mate or child

It is as outspoken as any poem in expressing disillusion with national leadership. The title suggests that the speaker represents the many whose lip-service submission to church and state can be simulated no longer. As with a short story, there is a final twist: the familiarised symbols of the atrocities of war – 'whips, gas-bombs, electric barbed wire' – are used for reverse effect: instead of rekindling the memories of First World War devastation, they are deployed to minimise past suffering in order to foreground the present tortures of social deprivation.

'Some Make This Answer'[12] and a 'Song for a Street-Song' were printed in *The Year's Poetry* 1936. Another of her poems, 'With All My Flesh', was included the previous year. The omission of Sylvia Townsend Warner from surveys of the Thirties is surprising when she was evidently published and when her preoccupations with politics, class and homosexual love link her to the young 'socialist poets'. Like Auden, she had a talent for music, moved from more metaphysical argument to a plainer speaking style and aimed to show that poetry was shaped both by tradition and its own generation 'a living and popular cultural tradition'.[13]

Like Auden's anthology, *The Poet's Tongue*, *Whether a Dove or a Seagull* – the shared collection with Valentine Ackland – did not give the separate authorships in order to encourage concentration on the poem rather than on the poet; a 'Note to the reader', which prefaces the book, stated:

> by withholding individual attributions, [the poets] hope that the freshness of anonymity will be preserved ... [it is] an experiment in the presentation of poetry and a protest against the frame of mind, too common, which judges the poem by the poet, rather than the poet by the poem.

Whether a Dove or a Seagull was a democratic project; it may also have been an attempt, on Sylvia Townsend Warner's part, to promote Valentine Ackland's poetry. Sylvia was conscious that her relative success as a writer overshadowed Valentine's. It was Sylvia who prepared Valentine's *Twenty Eight Poems* (1928) for private printing and it is possible that she suppressed her own poems out of sensitivity to Valentine's unrealised ambition to be a published poet.

The poems in *Whether a Dove or a Seagull* express the lesbian continuum of mutual love with subtle coding, as in the title poem: 'Whether a dove or a seagull lighted there/I cannot tell'.[14] There is nothing combative in the partnership, even when discussing its fluctuating moods. The shared battle is between celebrating or denying a desire which counters convention. The ambivalent gender of Sylvia Townsend Warner's love poetry is discussed by Jan Montefiore who perceives that under the guise of traditional form and the masculine pronoun in 'Drawing You, Heavy with Sleep', the poet plays with the complexities of female identity; the metaphors of fluidity and liquidity being unmistakable representations of female sexuality.[15]

Sylvia Townsend Warner was conscious of the double restraints of the lesbian existence and, of the pressures upon the single woman; she was also acutely aware of the frustrations of the housewife. In the following extract from an uncollected piece in *Time and Tide*, the looking-out-of-the window perspective is a literal device which punctuates the myth of domestic bliss; the view of the cottage may be idyllic to the outsider, but to the woman indoors the kitchen is a prison of overwork and confinement; this is the last of three stanzas:

> Yet if my rage
> Should smite away the cage
> If from the sea a wind should come
> And shout my jailors dumb,
> This heart that bangs on bone
> Tossed to the firmament of being alone,
> Would sink me like a stone.[16]

As a novelist and epistolist, Sylvia Townsend Warner has been noted for her wit, vigour and extraordinary range of tone. The small selection of her poems here barely indicates the extraordinary range of her versification and framework of reference. The enormity and diversity of the poetry can invite over-simplistic and summative generalisations. There are, however, common features which are a structural formality, whether ballad, lyric or burlesque, and the immediacy for which she aspired. Her talent for telling stories is applicable to her poetry: Glen Cavaliero detected her verbal economy, her embracing outlook and essential narrative skills: 'a tart unjudging awareness ... she knew how to hold attention.'[17]

Further Reading

Valentine Ackland, *For Sylvia: An Honest Account*, London, Chatto & Windus, 1985.

Barbara Brothers, 'Writing Against the Grain: Sylvia Townsend Warner and the Spanish Civil War' in Mary Lynn Broe and Angela Ingram, eds, *Women's Writing in Exile*, Chapel Hill, University of North Carolina Press, 1989, pp. 350–66.

Claire Harman, *Sylvia Townsend Warner: A Biography*, London, Chatto & Windus, 1985; London, Minerva, 1985.

Claire Harman, ed., *The Diaries of Sylvia Townsend Warner*, London, Chatto & Windus, 1994.

William Maxwell, ed., *The Letters of Sylvia Townsend Warner*, London: Chatto & Windus; New York, The Viking Press, 1982.

Wendy Mulford, *This Narrow Place: Sylvia Townsend Warner and Valentine Ackland ... Life, Letters and Politics 1930-1951*, London, Pandora, 1988.

Sylvia Townsend Warner, 'The Way By Which I Have Come', *Countryman*, xix, no. 2, 1939, pp. 472–86.

PN Review 23, vol. 8, no. 3, 1981, special edition on Sylvia Townsend Warner.

El Heroe

Nobody knew his name.
Pen nor paper will tell it.

We saw him rise up singing
Where the freshet leaps and fails.
5   With a gun at his shoulder,
Among the briars and brambles
His blue overalls
Were like a taunt sent ringing
Out to the eyes of the rebels.

10   The mountain wind arising
Keened all night for woe;

Midnight laid on his face
A handkerchief of snow;
Dawn came with a handful
15   Of woodland flowers to strow;
Like mourners through the hills
The freshets began to flow.

Nobody knew his name.
Pen nor paper will tell it.

Port Bou

Through these ruined walls
the unflawed sea.
And to the smell of sunned
earth and of salt
5   sea is added a third
smell that cries: Halt!
I am what will be

familiar to you
by this journey's end.
10   I am, stale, the smell
of the fire that quenched
the fire on this hearth, that brought
down these walls, that wrenched
this wound in the ground.

15   I am the smell
on all the winds of Spain.
I am the stink in the nostrils
of the men of Spain.
I have taken the place
25   of the incense at the burial,
I have usurped the breath
of the rose plucked for the bridal,
I am the odour of the wreath
that is held out for heroes
25   to behold and breathe.
I cordial the heart,
I refresh the brain,
I strengthen the resolved fury
of those who fight for Spain.

Journey To Barcelona

In that country pallor was from the ground,
darkness from the sky.
As the train took us by
we debated if it were mountain we saw or cloud.

5   The bleached fields are pallid as truth might be.
Men move on them like clouds.
Dwellings like hempen shrouds
wrap up squalor with a grave dignity.

Pale is that country like a country of bone.
10   Dry is the river-bed.
Darkness is overhead,
threatening with the fruitfulness implicit in storm.

The willows blanch, and catch their breath . . .
It rains in the hills!
15   The parched river-bed fills,
the sky thunders down fruitfulness.

Faithful to that earth the clouds are gathered again.
If the profile unknown
were cloud, it will be stone
before long. Rain from the red cloud, come to Spain!

Some Make This Answer

Unfortunately, he said, I have lost my manners.
That old civil twitch of visage and the retreat
Courteous of threatened blood to the heart, I cannot
Produce them now, or rig up their counterfeit.
5   Thrust muzzle of flesh, master, or metal, you are no longer
Terrible as an army with banners.

Admittedly on your red face or your metal proxy's
I read death, I decipher the gluttony to subdue
All that is free and fine, to savage it, knock it
10   About, taunt it to stupor, prison it life-through;
Moreover, I see you garnished with whips, gas-bombs, electric
    barbed wire,
And affable with church and state as with doxies.

But from other brows than yours I have felt a stronger

Voltage of death, walking among my fellow men
15 Have seen the free and the fine wasted with cold and hunger,
Diseased, maddened, death-in-life doomed, and the ten
Thousand this death can brag have reckoned against your
    thousand.
Shoddy king of terrors, you impress me no longer.

Song for a Street-Song

What, do you plan for children now?
A child is a pretty thing,
A thing of promise, a tender thing.
Day by day, year by year,
5 You love it more. War is near,
And dogs and strangers choking in the gas fume
Is a calmer spectacle than the fruit of the womb.
There's the sting
When the drums go rub-a-dub!
10 There's the rub!

What, do you plan for marriage now?
Love is a handsome thing,
A thing of tenderness, a growing thing.
Day by day, year by year,
15 It knits you more. War is near,
And flesh that lay beside you in marriage-bed
Mangles your own heart when it is ripped and shred.
There's the sting
When the drums go rub-a-dub!
20 There's the rub!

What, do you plan for freedom now?
Freedom is a noble thing,
The mind's sanction, a vital thing.
Day by day, year by year,
25 It claims you more. War is near,
And freedom in muck of warfare maimed and defiled
Is a bitterer hazard than loss of mate or child.
There's the sting
When the drums go rub-a-dub!
30 There's the rub!

We plan for love and children now,

And freedom, that noblest thing.
We gather to us everything
That's growing and tender, vital and dear,
35 To arm us more. War is near.
Against that enemy pang of the quickened sense
Is the swiftest weapon, is the surest defence.
There we cling
While the drums go rat-a-plan!
So we plan!

Drawing You, Heavy With Sleep

Drawing you, heavy with sleep to lie closer,
Staying your poppy head upon my shoulder,
It was as though I pulled the glide
Of a full river to my side.

5 Heavy with sleep and with sleep pliable
You rolled at a touch towards me. Your arm fell
Across me as a river throws
An arm of flood across meadows.

And as the careless water its mirroring sanction
10 Grants to him at the river's brim long stationed,
Long drowned in thought; that yet he lives
Since in that mirroring tide he moves,

Your body lying by mine to mine responded:
Your hair stirred on my mouth, my image was dandled
15 Deep in your sleep that flowed unstained
On from the image entertained.

Notes

1 Declaration of the Association of Writers in Defence of Culture, *Left Review*,
   vol. 1, no. 11, Aug. 1935, p. 462.
2 Valentine Cunningham, ed., *Spanish Front: Writers on the Civil War*, Oxford,
   Oxford University Press, 1986, p. xxxii.
3 Arnold Rattenbury, 'Plain Heart, Light Tether', *PN Review* 23, 1981, p. 46.
4 Louis Untermeyer, *CP*, p. xxiii.
5 'Benicasim', printed in *Left Review*, vol. 3, no. 14, March 1938, p. 841.
6 'Red Front', *Left Review*, vol. 1 no. 7, April 1935, p. 255; 'In This Midwinter',
   Left Review, vol. 1, no. 4, January 1935, p. 101.
7 Barbara Brothers, 'Writing Against the Grain: Sylvia Townsend Warner and
   the Spanish Civil War', pp. 350–66.
8 ibid., p. 351.

9 ibid., p. 361. Stephen Spender caricatured Sylvia Townsend Warner as the 'Lady Communist' in his memoir World Within World.

10 Sylvia Townsend Warner, 'The Way By Which I Have Come', p. 480.

11 ibid., p. 475.

12 'Some Make This Answer' was printed in Left Review, February 1936, p. 214.

13 W.H. Auden, The Poet's Tongue, discussed in Samuel Hynes, The Auden Generation, London, The Bodley Head, 1979, p. 166.

14 See section on Valentine Ackland for the whole poem 'Whether a dove or a seagull lighted there'.

15 Jan Montefiore, Feminism and Poetry, London, Pandora, 1987, p. 158.

16 'Seaside Cottage', Time and Tide, 12 August, 1933, p. 960.

17 Glen Cavaliero, 'The Short Stories', PN Review 23, 1981, p. 45.

19
Dorothy Wellesley
1889–1956

1920 *Poems*, privately printed
1926 *Genesis: An Impression*, London, Heinemann
1930 *Deserted House: A poem sequence*, London, Hogarth
1934 *Poems of Ten Years*, London, Macmillan
1936 *Selections from the Poems of Dorothy Wellesley*, London, Macmillan
1942 *The Last Planet and Other Poems*, London, Hogarth
1946 *Desert Wells: New Poems*, London, Michael Joseph
1948 *Selections from the Poems of Dorothy Wellesley*, London, Williams & Norgate
1954 *Rhymes for Middle Years*, London, Barrie
1955 *Early Light: The Collected Poems of Dorothy Wellesley*, London, Hart Davis

Dorothy Ashton was educated by a governess, married Lord Gerald Wellesley in 1914 and had two children; she became Duchess of Wellington in 1943 although by that time she lived apart from her husband. She features substantially in the correspondence between Vita Sackville-West and Virginia Woolf and appears to have been used by each of them to kindle jealousy in the other. 'Dottie' was a confidante to both Harold and Vita concerning the insecurities in their relationship, and she in her turn became increasingly dependent upon Vita after her own marriage had dissolved in 1923. In 1928, she bought a house in Sussex which she shared with Hilda Matheson, also a friend and lover of Vita's. Dorothy travelled with Vita and she also separately visited several countries including Italy, Crete, Egypt and India. She began writing and publishing before the First World War and continued throughout her life. She was particularly productive in the 1930s when she became established in literary circles, even though Edith Sitwell was dismissive of her. She invested money in the Woolfs' Hogarth Press and edited the Hogarth Living Poets series and *A Broadcast Anthology of Modern Poetry* (Hogarth Press) in 1930. Several of her poems were selected for *The Oxford Book of Modern Verse* (1936) and in his broadcast lecture of the same year, W.B. Yeats cited her poem 'Matrix' as exemplary of modern poetry. In spite of the promotion by Yeats and her lack of financial worries, she knew the encumbrances of a woman writer, 'if I were a man, and had a wife to take practical life off my shoulders, I might start the inner life again'.[1]

'Mother' is a woman's monologue which curses the biological determinism of women throughout the ages. The simultaneous evocation of antiquity and the brave twentieth century world is effective in this poem which typically combines symbols of bygone, often prehistoric, epochs with a modern directness of address. Dorothy Wellesley was certainly not a traditionalist; in *The Dictionary of National Biography*, Vita Sackville-West describes her as a 'natural rebel, rejecting all conventions ... a proclaimed agnostic'.[2]

In 'Avebury', the poet draws upon pagan symbols to articulate the nihilism which is often associated with the atmosphere at the outbreak of the Second World War. Certainly, Dorothy Wellesley's have the energy of many contemporaneous poems of this time which suggest that the onset of war had once again provided new material for writing. The simultaneous longing for and rejection of faith is a frequent tension in Second World War verse. The accelerations and the pregnant halts in rhythm capture the co-existent panic and despair which connect the mood of the imminent war to that of pre-scientific and prehistoric savagery: the god of war is seen to have triumphed over the god of technological progress. The recurring theme, then, is the end-of-the-decade disillusion with man-made developments. Classical and Biblical myths are co-mingled in order to examine and expose ancient ways of imposing some order on a chaotic and mystifying universe. In 'The Enemy', the poet resurrects images from First World War poetry in order to confront the spiritual regress of mankind – 'the nations are bombing the cemeteries of the slain'.

There is little subtlety or undertone in Dorothy Wellesley's poems. Their force is in the speaker's aggression which W.B. Yeats found unusual in a woman; Yeats, whilst recognising the unevenness of her achievements – 'at times facile and clumsy, at times magnificent in her masculine rhythm' – most admired the 'precision' of her style and her ability to make 'changes in pace'.[3] Otherwise, very little has been written about her poems. Vita Sackville-West thought that the loose versification was undisciplined and denounced her as, 'a born romantic ... [her] intellectual powers did not equal her imagination.'[4] Geoffrey Grigson, reviewing *Poems of Ten Years* in *The Criterion*, used her as an example of women who were unschooled in verse writing;[5] a more attentive reviewer of the *Selections* acknowledged her limited technical range, but also noted her 'delicate gift for telling a story in verse' ... and 'an infinite capacity for recording detail with exquisite definition'.[6]

Further Reading

Dorothy Wellesley, *Far Have I Travelled*, London, James Barrie, 1952.
Dorothy Wellesley, ed., *Letters on Poetry from W.B. Yeats to Dorothy Wellesley*, Oxford, Oxford University Press, 1940; new edition, ed. Kathleen Raine, 1964.

Mother

Woman, thou shalt say to son:
'I, the blood, got thee upon
Nothing but a phallic stone.
This, no more – a phallic stone.

5   Now I wait your probable death,
I, who was a fact of earth,
Never held a fainting faith
In Buddha or in Christ's belief.

Life is naught but bitter moan
10   Got upon an ancient stone.'

Some such curse the woman hath.

June 1939

The Enemy

There is some delight in bombing an Enemy
Whom all mankind must hate.
There is some foresight in reading the Tarot card
These years ago over an adversary.
5   There is splendour in the pride and fury of the pard.

But now the hour is late,
We must fold up the chess-board,
And set the cards aside,
For now stand up the spectres of eventide.

10   What are these forms in Flanders I behold
From Ypres and from the Saar?
What is this clanking of young bones, now old?
Why do the stars shudder
As never shuddered a star?

15   It is because the bombs are opening the cemeteries.
As at the twilight of the Crucifixion

The tombs shall open and give forth their dead
Of those who died for liberty, in their affliction.

They shall be bombed once more,
20   Wake from the only sleep that man can gain.
Millions of men are risen of the slain,
Who remember maybe the ships only,
The dusk, the lights along the English shore.

They shall rise out of earth,
25   Most trusty of their worth,
Their spiritual power most infinite and plain
Who asked no profit from their death
And from the rich no gain.

They rise most wise with shining eyes
30   Who begged no gold for pain.

With unperturbed faith
They rise from earth
Who have no more to lose, nothing to gain.
Their childhood passed like sunlight
35   Through the April-beaten rain.

Unhappy Enemy, the ghosts of the young
Are terrible to see
Who come, roused up from their last sleep
To meet again with broken bone
40   The harried hunted mind of man with soul of stone,
Their unpitying hearts withered completely away.

The dark comes down, it is the end of day,
Hark to the hosts of ghosts
Of unapparent tread
45   Who have been called too early from their bed.
Kill off the living, Enemy!
For you have raised the dead.
They come with clanging sound, and phosphorescent eyes,
With the worm that never dies,
50   They rise, they rise, who care no more for pain!
Pale Enemy, hail!
The nations are bombing the cemeteries of the slain.

September 1939

Avebury

Their skulls were more beautiful than ours,
Their teeth finer, greater their fighting powers,
The cavities of their eyes beheld such skies,
Such trees, such flowers,
5   At which we in our infancy wonder;
The cavities of those great eyes knew all
That man can know.
And I think that those who wrote their runes
Were older than their stones.

10   For the wise are destroyed by fools.

As the same end comes ever
As to the wise men of Avebury,
I do not know if the wise men,
Who wrote runes on the stones
15   With flint tools,
Are of any worth to humanity.

For the wise are destroyed by fools.

I do not believe,
Musing on Socrates and his great wisdom,
20   And the Alexandrian schools,
That wise men are worth survival.
I see only in the dusk of these great stones
That the wise are destroyed by fools.

These great stones
25   Lead up to a temple all men have forgotten,
Since all mankind comes to the same end,
Leaving in Egypt a little, in England nothing;

I have no faith in the wisdom of the ancients begotten,
Do not believe in the wise men of Avebury,
30   For the wise are without worth
On an earth destroyed by fools.

I think that the wise men of Avebury
Are better left unborn;
I think that those who wrote runes on the stones,
35   Intoning at evening, labouring at dawn,
Knew this also.

Yet I hail the law of intellectual constancy!
The man who tamed, not by chance, the fire,
The man who invented the wheel,
40 The man who first feared the moon,
Writing her madness in a rune,
In the man who first named a star.

I believe in the agony, in the sweat of the wise,
And in the crucifixion of Solomon.

1939

April 1939

Judas Iscariot looks down from heaven
To see the region where Jesus is driven,
Jesus Christ looks up from the place
To stare Iscariot in the face.

Notes

1 Dorothy Wellesley, Letter to Yeats, *The World Split Open*, ed. Louise Bernikow, London, The Women's Press, 1979, p. 162.
2 Vita Sackville-West, Victoria Glendinning, *Vita: The Life of Vita Sackville-West*, London, Weidenfeld & Nicolson, 1983, p. 113.
3 W.B. Yeats, Introduction to *The Oxford Book of Modern Verse*, Oxford, Oxford University Press, (1936) 1937, pp. xxxii–xxxiv. See also, W.B. Yeats, Introduction to *Selections from the Poems of Dorothy Wellesley*, 1948, originally written 1936.
4 Victoria Glendinning, *Vita*, p. 113.
5 Geoffrey Grigson, 'Books of the Quarter', *The Criterion*, vol. iv, no. 54, October 1934, pp. 141–3.
6 Review of *Selections*, *Time and Tide*, 15 August 1936, vol. xvii, p. 1156.

20
Anna Wickham
1884–1947

1911 *Songs*, John Oland, privately printed
1915 *The Contemplative Quarry*, London, The Poetry Bookshop
1916 *The Man with a Hammer*, London, Grant & Richards
1921 *The Little Old House*, London, The Poetry Bookshop
1936 *Anna Wickham: Richards Shilling Selections*, London, Richards Press
1971 *Selected Poems by Anna Wickham*, London, Chatto & Windus
1984 *The Writings of Anna Wickham: Free Woman and Poet*, ed. R. D. Smith, London, Virago

Edith Alice Mary Hepburn, née Harper, assumed the pseudonym 'John Oland' for her first book and subsequently adopted 'Anna Wickham' as her professional title. Born in Wimbledon, her family emigrated in 1900 to Australia where she was educated at schools which included two Roman Catholic convents and Sidney High School for Girls. She returned to England at the age of 20, married two years later, had four children, was separated in 1926 and rejoined her husband just before his death from a climbing accident in 1929.

Anna Wickham resented having to give up her career as an opera singer in order to be a wife and mother. She felt stifled by the Victorian professional middle-class conventions of her husband's family, by their disdain for the poor and by their disapproval of rights for women. Her husband had inherited his parents' suspicion of the arts and dismissed her to a private asylum when she published *Songs* in 1911. Her memoirs tell of her continual conflicts between a sense of duty to her family and her own need for imaginative freedom. The poem 'Dilemma' expresses the agony of choosing between safe but self-destructive social respectability and the more risky personal liberty. For Anna Wickham, this dilemma was never resolved and she suffered from severe guilt when her third son died in 1921, regretting that her writing had diverted her from family responsibilities. In 1935, she recorded her determination to free herself from this guilt-laden past:

> It is the fourth of March, 1935 ... 29 years attempting to order the house. For 25 years of my misery, it has been my passionate preoccupation ... the shades of the

> prison house began to close in on me. My husband ... from being my devoted
> lover seemed to become my enemy and my judge.[1]

The remorse and weariness were never expunged. According to the eldest son, James, the reasons for his mother's suicide were exhaustion and the belief that her children could do, and would do, better without her.[2]

Anna Wickham was a prolific poet: before the First World War she produced 900 poems in four years; many of these and much of her correspondence were destroyed during the Second World War, but there remained nevertheless 1,100 unpublished poems, in addition to the published collections. Her work cannot readily be categorised, and she herself was something of a maverick by dint of her upbringing and intellectual restlessness:

> Her Australian childhood offered freedoms unavailable to English women, and it
> seems to have stamped her as well with a robust sense of sexual entitlement, a
> view of social inequality and an authentic personal voice, all of which set her
> apart from other women poets of the period.[3]

She came into contact with individuals from different social and literary circles; her friends included T.E. Hulme, Dylan Thomas and D.H. Lawrence. In Paris, she fell under the influence of Natalie Barney and met many writers from the United States, including Djuna Barnes and Ezra Pound. The room at 'Bon Secours' in 'Pilgrimage' presumably symbolises the sexual freedom which was more available abroad.

During the 1930s, a widow with three children, Anna Wickham needed to make money from her poems. The 1936 Richards Shilling collection contained 36 poems, 30 of which were new. It was edited by the poet Fytton Armstrong, under the pseudonym of John Gawsworth, who also included her work in *Edwardian Poetry* and *Neo-Georgian Poetry*, both published in 1937. According to R.D. Smith, in the second half of the decade she was helped by 'the violent changes in poetic fashion brought about by Auden', and began to have a revival.[4] She developed an international reputation as a poet and Louis Untermeyer helped to promote her work in America where many anthologies included more poems of hers than of the major poets.[5] In 1938, supported by seven feminists, she drew up the manifesto, *The League for the Protection of the Imagination of Women*. In 1939 she would have appeared on BBC television had not war been declared.

R.D. Smith deduces that the voice of the poems is unmistakably the poet's and that poetry was the substitute for her sacrificed singing career. The singer, however, is usually fictional. The dramatic force of the poems can be misleading in giving the *impression* of spontaneous self-expression: the spontaneity is, however, a cleverly constructed immediacy. Anna Wickham was intensely self-critical and constantly reworked her poems. Her musical training enabled her to have an ear for rhythm and movement, although she eschewed the formal patterns of British poetry on account of their associations with traditionalism and because they impeded the simulation of free speech. Her early poetry is often experimental and sometimes cluttered with rhyme and assonance until she solved the dual demands of form and freedom with the 'perfection of imperfection', like the near perfect or 'faulty rhyme'.[6] The poet draws upon literary inheritances which are shared by all cultural echelons – ballad, pastoral, fairy tale, and folk legend – to challenge their assumptions and to upturn stereotypes. It is often the symbols of the heroic which are affronted, as in 'King Alfred and the Peasant Woman', and 'Lament of the Red Knight'. The betrayal and misuse of women is a dominant motif: 'The Boor's Wooing' is the song of the chivalric lover who will turn his beautiful bride into a servant wife. 'The Sportsman', 'Pugilist' and 'The Happy Mathematician' are jibes at stereo- typed masculinity. 'Love Song' is structurally ironic in the quatrains of classic love poetry which are injected with the unashamed proclamations of the woman whose sexual desires will be met and then discarded by her lover. Women are presented as both victims and winners in 'Song of the Lonely Shepherd' where the rescued damsel has asserted her independence. In 'Song of Ophelia the Survivor', there is an ambiguity about the idealised mutuality of what could-have-been. This poem was first published by Richards in *Edwardian Poetry* with all six verses, but the last was dropped in *Richards Shilling Selection* and was not picked up by Virago in *Writings*, although it does appear in the *Selected Poems* (1971).[7]

In rejecting conventional codes of masculinity and femininity, Anna Wick- ham's heroes and heroines are the unnamed and unsung who are consigned to drab urban monotony: 'Alas! For all the pretty women who marry dull men, / Go into the suburbs and never come out again',[8] or:

> I feel I must sob or shriek
> To force a man of the Croydon class
> To live or to love or to speak[9]

The mixture of the conversational and the lyrical imperceptibly contrasts the idealised and mythical with quotidian realities. Anna Wickham is at her best in telling the story of women whose masks of ordinariness and survival conceal frustration and a losing battle with pain; the few lines of 'The Sick Assailant' encapsulate the whole life of the woman who is physically and mentally assaulted. Harold Monro was one of the first to spot her 'rare power of condensing a troublesome problem of social psychology into the form of a lyric'.[10] It is possible that the corporal punishment of her childhood followed by repression within marriage account for the recurrence of images of beating.[11] The poems of the 1936 collection also contain frequent images of horse-riding where the man is usually in the saddle.

The poems here are all taken from *Richards Shilling Selection* of 1936 but it is possible that one or two may have been composed before 1930. The following extract from 'The Explanation' (undated) is in keeping with the style and sentiments of Anna Wickham's poems in the 1920s and 1930s and is evidence that the oldest poet of the 1930s was sensitive to the prejudices against the woman poet:

It's so, good Sirs, a Woman-poet sings,
Sick self, and not exterior things,
She'd joy enough in flowers, and lakes and light,
Before she won soul's freedom in a fight.
Thus half creation is but half expressed . . .[12]

The Sick Assailant

I hit her in the face because she loved me.
It was the challenge of her faithfulness that
        moved me –
For she knew me, every impulse, every mood,
As if my veins had run with her heart's blood.
5   She knew me, every damned incontinence,
Yet she forbore with her accursed meekness.
I could have loved her had she ever blamed me,
It was her sticky, irritating patience shamed me.
I was tired-sick. It was her business to amuse me:
10   Her faith could only daunt me and confuse me.
She was a fine great wench, and well I knew
She was one good half panther, one half shrew –
Then why should my love, more than any other,
Induce in her the silly human Mother?
15   She would have nursed me, bathed me, fed me,

She delivered me her soul to thaw me – she'd
        have married me!
I hit her in the face because she loved me.
It was her sticky, irritating Patience moved me.

The Silent Singer

I have no words that could prevail
Against the furies of my male.
When we go out I come behind,
While he expounds his angry mind:

5   O I walk humbly in the path
Of his just wrath!
Then he goes singing –

Sings like a mavis, or a boy,
From a still secret source of joy;
10 And I am all humility,
His pleasure's me.
Silent I follow many a mile –
Trying my hardest not to smile –
To my heart's singing.

The Dilemma

If he roam far away
From the herd's track,
He may run mad one day
And not come back.

5   If he feed where he stands,
He will find nothing strange nor sweet:
He must die in home lands
Because he cannot eat.

Pilgrimage

I think of the room at Bon Secours:
The clock on the shelf, and the bare-board floor,
The tallow smell from the out-blown light,
And the laughter and love of the prodigal night:
5   I wish we were young, dear,
As young and as poor
As when we stole Heaven
At Bon Secours.

The Boor's Wooing

I love her for her fine blue coat,
And for that ivory at her throat
All cut about in charming shapes,
Small flowers, and nests, and birds and grapes.

5   I love her for her white, deft hands.

With what an art, she smooths the strands
Of Chloe's hair to make a seemliness
Among the gins of that sweet-scented wilderness!

But most, I love the farmwoman who drowses
10   While my fine lady walks the dim-lit houses:
And by my head! that canny wench shall wake
And laugh and labour for her peasant's sake.

When first I saw her in her painted room
My unskilled silence spoke her doom.
15   What call had I to waste my power in speech
When what I willed was still beyond my reach?

But I have cut a rope from the tough vine,
And I've distilled a draught more strong than wine.
First she shall drink, and then I'll draw her hence,
20   To pin an apron on her elegance.

And she shall kilt her skirt, and bare her arms,
And live about my fields, and on my farms.
Is she thin Venus on a painted fan?
No! she's right woman, and Myself's her man!

King Alfred and the Peasant Woman

Threw me from the house, did he?
Well, to new chivalry that is no great thing!
I am my father's daughter, Lady,
And he's a pretty figure in the ring.

5   But my man, my master, there he sat a-dreaming,
While all the house might burn, and he'd not sorrow;
Nor had I any warrant that his scheming
Would bring us any victory on the morrow.

And I spoke to him – O I informed him!
10   He'd be a dead man, if he were not stung.
Could any man keep hands down, and me lashing?
Ach, you insult my tongue!

I'd rather he fought me than missed his combats,
Though I'm not built for blows upon the heart.
15   Give me a breastplate and I'll at 'em –
Though that's fool-woman's part!

[170]

I love him, and if he comes back with honour,
After the fight I drove him to is won,
He'll find his woman, with her glory on her:
  Please God, the child's a son!

Lament of the Red Knight

Tree-blossom and May
Are vanished away;
The mad merry month is over.
Alas! and alas!
5   How came it to pass
Not all that month was I any woman's lover?

The Queen sits up in her sullen bower;
Her eyes shoot wrath like darts from a tower.
Such a melancholy harridan never was seen!
10   But alas! and alas! I love the Queen.
Now I must bear Winter to every warm glade;
For never again will I kiss a young maid.

Song of the Lonely Shepherd

(WRITTEN FOR MME NICKLASS KEMPNER)

I found her asleep in the snows:
Her head and her feet were bare,
And she was like a wild sweet rose
By miracle flung there.
5   I carried her in to my love and my rest,
And I thawed her feet at my breast.

And all the winter long
She neither spoke nor stirred:
My heart made a happy song
10   (O I was blithe as a bird!):
'There'll be an end to these bitter days;
I'll see her dance down flowery ways.'

And on an April morning,
Alas! I was early abroad
15   To pluck a crown for adorning
The head that my soul adored –

[171]

Alas and alas! I was home too late:
The cruel feet had danced out through my gate.

O little feet, matched like two happy lovers,
20   Have you no pity on me?
Know ye not that this sheepskin covers
Sore wounds, and my piteous misery?
Your ice has burned a brand on my breast;
Then lead her back, to my love and my rest!

Song of Ophelia the Survivor

There is no smirch of sin in you, only its fires.
You are a man burned white with merciless desires;
A restless heat consumes you, and your brain,
Tortured to torturing, craves for ugly pain.

5   Beauty still lives in you, and from her seat
Controls your glances, and directs your feet;
One look from you taught me so much of love,
I have all pleasure, just to watch you move.

That look was like a wet blue mist of flowers,
10   Which held compelling loveliness and sleepy powers.
I dreamed of calling pipes down a warm glade;
By the transposed music of your soul I was betrayed.

Pipe for me, my dear lover! I will come,
And your sick soul shall find in me a home;
15   It will be your house, clean, high, and strong.
And You shall live in me, all winter long.

As you are fevered, I will be a pool,
Full of green shadows, level, silent, cool.
You shall bathe in me, in my being move;
20   Will put out your fires with my strong love.

A thousand changes shall my love reveal
And all its changes shall have power to heal,
And in the end we'll be as we began:
I will be simple woman, you my man.

The Sportsman

I'm watching my power and my rapture
Go by me like leaves on a wind:

If I held up my hand, I could capture
And hold them – if I had the mind.
5   Is it Hell that I fear for my soul,
Or Heaven I'd come to at length?
No! I'm staking to-day on Control!
I'm backing an ultimate Strength!

Pugilist) Boxed

Though I am well-clothed, well-booted, and well-fed,
I yet have the hunger of Hell in me
For a dream that is dead;
And that, though I have gained two grades in rank,
5   Have a horse, and a house, and gold in the bank.
My mind is dull with fullness, yet I know
I have one utter need –
To find a foe!
I will strip off this fine constricting coat
10   And grip Necessity by his thin throat.

The Happy Mathematician

(AN ARITHMETIC LESSON FOR A SMALL BOY: WRITTEN FOR
JOHN UNTERMEYER)

When he was nine, he thought he knew
All about two times two.
He sang his tables out aloud
And he was very glad and proud.
5   He thought: 'I'll not be weak or poor,
Because twice two are always four:
I know this now, and I'll get knowledge
Even more fine, when I'm at college.'

When he was ninety-nine or more,
10   Wise Death came knocking at his door.
Death said: 'As you get nearer Heaven,
Twice two are five or six or seven;
And at the centre of God's heart,
The whole is as the smallest part.'
15   The old man laughed: 'That interests me.
Teach me your tables, Death,' said he.

Notes

1 Anna Wickham, 'Fragment of an Autobiography', R.D. Smith, ed., *The Writings of Anna Wickham: Free Woman and Poet*, London, Virago, 1984, p. 45.

2 *Writings*, p. xxiii.

3 Celeste Schenck, 'Anna Wickham', *The Gender of Modernism*, ed. Bonnie Kime Scott, Bloomington, Indiana University Press, 1990, p. 164.

4 R.D. Smith, *Writings*, p. 27.

5 ibid., p. 23.

6 'The Egoist', *SP*, 1971, p. 25.

7 I am grateful to James Hepburn for this information.

8 'Meditation at Kew', *Writings*, p. 45.

9 'Nervous Prostration', *SP*, 1971, p. 20.

10 Harold Monro, *Some Contemporary Poets*, London, Simpkin & Marshall, 1920, p. 196.

11 See R.D. Smith, *Writings*, p. 43.

12 'The Explanation', *SP*, 1971, p. 32.

21
The Listener

The Listener did more for the new poetry of the Thirties than did *New Writing* or *Left Review*, but the contribution is best measured in terms of the number of poets brought before a wide audience. ... It brought [these poets] before the main body of the intelligent reading public which the little magazines with their circulation in the hundreds, did not reach.[1]

In 1929, *The Listener*, the British Broadcasting Corporation's weekly publication, launched itself into a 'new venture': it declared its aims as the education and entertainment of its readers and to respond to the constant demands for the text of broadcast talks after delivery. Radio was important to the cultural divergences of the 1930s as it was a new acquisition in many homes, and consequently, the most influential link between people; it had the potential to also bridge social divides in reaching into the 'homes and hearts' of north and south and of being equally accessible to readers and non-readers. It was, therefore, a major marketing vehicle; in 1938, the poet Herbert Read wrote to the new Director of the BBC to say that the future of poetry was in his hands: 'Poetry is ceasing to be printed; poetry is no longer read ... it is in the power of the radio to revive poetry as the spoken art.'[2] He saw a return to oral verse and public performance as vital to preserving the poet's position. The radio did, in fact, reach thousands, both at home and away.

The extent of the audience reached by airwaves and the range of poetry which was evidently available and appealing, support the conspectus that many more poets were writing and being read in the 1930s than have usually been represented. Although an Establishment institution, the editorship was arguably more inclusive, less xenophobic, and less misogynist than the allegedly non-partisan *New Verse*. It broadcast older and a host of younger poets, poetry from America, and translations of European poets. Julian Symons, W.H. Auden, C. Day-Lewis, Stephen Spender or Michael Roberts are less visible presences than Clifford Dyment, Richard Church, Richard Goodman, A.S.J. Tessimond or Lilian Bowes Lyon. The women who most often had poems printed in *The Listener* were Vita Sackville-West, Frances Cornford and K.J. Raine.

Many articles are in keeping with the self-analysing tendencies of the decade. The poet laureate, John Masefield, called for young poets to 'create the new poetry for the new audience'.[3] There are several articles on modern poetry by poets and critics. In common, they acknowledge the fashion for individualism and for constructing the impression of a speaking voice: 'This conversationality and directness of appeal is a mark of a good deal of modern poetry, as a large proportion of the poems we have published weekly in these pages will testify.'[4] In addition, the preferences for imitating speech rhythms made modern poetry particularly suitable for reading aloud. The question of literary value was both a concern of and an opportunity for the paper's central interest in the relationship between poetry and the public: 'The poems we publish may vary widely in quality, but we firmly believe they deserve and demand this kind [unprejudiced and informed] of reading.'[5]

The poems here are included, therefore, because they were approved, published and widely read or heard. Margaret Stanley-Wrench was an undergraduate at Somerville College, Oxford and was also one of the few women to appear in *Oxford Poetry* (1936). She won the Newdigate Prize for English Verse in 1937 with 'The Man in The Moon' which was subsequently printed in periodicals and anthologies. It may raise questions about the criteria for prizewinning, but it was nevertheless an achievement. After that she had several poems published in *Time and Tide* and her first book of poems was published in 1938.[6] She seems to have written her best work during the 1950s.

Some measure of the success of *The Listener* in engaging with its public is indicated in the number of entries to its poetry competition in 1933 – eleven thousand, thirty of which were found to be 'of interest and merit'. Six of the winning poems were by women, one of whom was Jan Struther.[7] During the 1930s, Jan Struther wrote columns describing the fictional life of a 'Mrs Miniver' which were turned into a best-seller and a Hollywood film.[8] Her poems were printed in the *Spectator*, *London Mercury* and *Best Poetry* anthologies. Jan Struther's poem 'Lament In Spring' is like others of the period which attempt to respond to the troubles of 1936. There are dreamlike aspects in Winifred Welles' parodic love poem 'White Valentine' which seems to be an emblem of truce in a rocky relationship.

At the beginning of the decade, Vita Sackville-West was commissioned as a reviewer by one of her lovers Hilda Matheson, who was Director of Talks at the BBC until 1932. Other women were involved in *The Listener* in reviewing, being reviewed and writing articles. There were undoubtedly more than first appears, because the prevalent use of initials often disguises the gender of the author. When Janet Adam Smith became assistant editor of the magazine, she was praised for spotting and aiding the young talent of the day and in *Poems of Tomorrow* (1935), which she had selected from *The Listener*, she faithfully represented the spectrum of poetry read on the radio, but, surprisingly, was cautious over including women.

Margaret Stanley-Wrench

The Man in the Moon

FROM THE NEWDIGATE PRIZE POEM 1937

And they have said there is a man in the moon,
Watching eternally, sleepless and undying,
Condemned for sin to hold his icy realm
To see no spring, inherit no fresh green,
5   Nor feel the lusty sun nor the blown rain.
They have peopled that unwavering deceit
Of ivory light, the borrower, the moon,
Being fearful of the empty shaft of space;
They strut upon their petty earth,
10 And see themselves upon the stars
Who sullenly ignore this earth, and stare
In polished insolence through night.
For man, though in his mind the king of space,
Shrinks lonely, terror in the compass of his shadow,
15 Birds fly before him, mice, prick-eyed with fear,
Peer from the boles of trees. No feet by his shall tread,
The light-foot hooves of deer have fled,
And though he tame the stallion's burning crest,
And hood the hawk, they fear him, and keep close
20 Their knowledge and their love. So, in his loneliness
Man multiplies himself, the silent trees
At night step dryads, the unwavering brooks
Become the silver-haired, the crystal nymphs,
Birds hide a ravished girl, a god treads golden
25 In the brief sunlight of an April day.

28 July 1937

Jan Struther

Lament in Spring

Not much longer now
Will the eye see
Bonework of bole and bough,
The beautiful, austere

5   Essentials of the tree;
Intricate tracery
Upward and outward growing
From strength to filigree;
Inverted river, flowing
10   Backward from sea to hills,
Back through a hundred streams, a thousand rills.

Already now the year
Has chimed a quarter;
Nights than days are shorter;
15   Leaf-time is almost here.
Soon an extravagant folly,
Impetuous, unruly,
Will mask this fine
20   Sureness and grace of line;
Soon a green fever
Will rage unchecked, and cover
With quick confusion clarity,
With sweet lies, verity.

Nothing to do but wait,
25   Endure this wild invasion,
This blurring of the vision,
This tumult of the heart:
Knowing that, soon or late,
Autumn with pain, weeping and stormy splendour
30   Will bring once more
Mind's sanity,
Heart's candour;
And trees stand brave and bare,
Stripped of green vanity.

27 May 1936

Winifred Welles

White Valentine

Since you are dead, and I am gone,
And that old house we knew now known
Only to strangers, I will cut
A paper heart for you, and put
5   A picture in its centre. Faint,

And delicate, and small, I'll paint
Two figures there, and they will be
A miniature of you and me.
We're by my long, gold mirror; bright
10 The bitter afternoon's cold light
Comes thinly through the window pane
And strikes across us. A fine skein
Of leafless boughs and twigs is drawn
Across the sky. On the white lawn,
15 Their shadows in an intricate net
Are with a clear precision set.
It's Winter, and we are at home
Together in my pale blue room.
There you, a gaunt boy, gravely stand,
20 Sedately moving your thin hand.
I am the tall child in the chair,
Letting you brush my long, light hair.

Upon this shape of brittle lace
And gentle tints, there is no place
25 For the crude colour of the heart.
There is a pastel day, apart
From all the later sombre years,
The spite, mistrust, the sullen tears
And sad; from the crouched attitudes
30 Of separate terrors, from the feuds
Shameful and harsh, between a brother
And sister close to one another,
But cleaved as woman and as man;
From all the honoured daily plan,
35 That was the falsely mutual life
Of two not husband and not wife,
Caught frantic in a marriage mesh,
Which was of blood but not of flesh.
All that's their book, closed now forever,
40 This but a picture for the cover.

So, on my fragile valentine,
Let not one stain fall from that vine
Which, in the temples and the wrists,
Distorted, deviously, twists;
45 Not one drop spatter from that flood,
Which is the dense and scalding blood.

Here, decorated in white lace, –
We share an instant all of grace,
And tenderness, and innocence.

50 Briefly, but ever, here relents
All taut devotion. On this heart,
We live released in trivial art,
Lovely, naive –
It's winter weather,
And we are in my room together,
55 Amused, at peace; I in my chair,
You standing, brushing my long hair.

25 August 1938

Notes

1 A.T. Tolley, *The Poetry of the Thirties*, London, Gollancz, 1975, pp. 120, 121.
2 Herbert Read, 'An Open Letter', *New Verse*, nos. 31–2, Autumn, 1938, p. 10.
3 'A Letter from the Poet Laureate', 24 December 1930, p. 1052.
4 Editorial, 11 January 1933.
5 Editorial, 12 July 1933.
6 Margaret Stanley-Wrench, *Newsreel and other Poems*, London, Macmillan, 1938; *A Tale for the Fall of the Year and Other Poems*, London, Linden Press, 1959.
7 Jan Struther, 'The Glass Blower', *Listener*, 26 July 1933, p. 109.
8 See Alison Light, *Forever England: Femininity, Literature and Conservatism Between the Wars*, London, Routledge, 1991, pp. 11–12.

22
Time and Tide
1920–1976

Time and Tide was a weekly journal of articles, essays, reviews and letters. Its first editor and founder, Helen Archdale, was succeeded by the millionairess Lady Rhondda who, according to Vera Brittain, was the only woman editor of a weekly paper and 'concealed a forceful personality behind a façade of shyness'.[1] Lady Margaret Rhondda had intended it to be primarily a political review which would influence influential people. Ideologically liberal, it claimed to be 'the review with independent news' and thrived in spite of the recession. It was particularly successful during the 1920s and 1930s. It modelled itself on the format of the *New Statesman* but had a clear commitment to women's issues. It printed contributions by both sexes, but the editors evidently encouraged women at all stages of its production. During the 1930s, it was as equally devoted to the arts and feminist activities as to national and international affairs. The editorial openness to discussions about gender can be assumed by its reputation and by the printing of articles such as 'The University Idea' by Vera Brittain,[2] about the need for equal access to degrees; it published other reports and correspondence on women's continuing attempts to achieve greater freedoms, as in the 'Oxford Union Divorce Debate' when the motion to allow divorce after three years' separation was carried.[3] Such articles on changing gender roles are further verification that women's rights and the meaning of 'Equality' were still central concerns of women in the decade. Lady Rhondda herself was active in trying to procure the vote for women under 30, through such initiatives as the Six Point Group and Equal Rights International.

One leading contributor to *Time and Tide* was E.M. Delafield who wrote a stimulating 'Women in Fiction' series, although her poetry was rather trite.[4] Of the women mentioned in this anthology, Winifred Holtby, Frances Cornford, Naomi Mitchison, Edith Sitwell and Sylvia Townsend Warner regularly contributed poems, articles, and reviews; Gwen Raverat published woodcuts and reviews; there were letters from Edith Sitwell and Laura Riding as well as Winifred Holtby, who was Lady Rhondda's youngest director on a Board of Directors which included Cicely Hamilton and Rebecca West; E.J. Scovell was an assistant editor and a reviewer of books during the Thirties. On average, *Time and Tide* printed one poem a week.

I have selected poems by women who seem to have had several poems published in this and other journals. Stella Gibbons (1902–1989) is known as a novelist – she was a prolific prose writer – but also published collections of poetry in 1930, 1934, 1938 and 1951.[5] Her poems tend to be pastoral lyrics which attempt to connect to a bygone golden age. 'Continuity' starts off with some recognition of the contemporary world but it is not 'modern' in that there are no mixed feelings about contrasting the warring present with a supposedly peaceful past. Freda C. Bond's poems were printed in periodicals like *Country Life* and *Best Poetry* annual anthologies. 'Pity Wasted' is an individual and independent response to the modern world, especially to divisions of class. The rhythms construct the measures of speech, although not evenly. The incongruity of the archaic vocabulary and the contemporary context is not a deliberate blending of old or new; it is accidentally anachronistic in the clash between outmoded language and the attempt at immediacy. 'After the War' needs to be recast for more poetic subtlety, but it demonstrates that women shared the growing disillusion and nihilism of the decade. The last stanza is a reminder that colonial pride had not been quite extinguished in 1935.

'The Last Prayer' is a poem of protest, couched under a cover of cheerful stoicism. The suppression of the wish for a partner is more of a *cri de cœur* than the jolly iambics suggest. The question marks, exclamation points and ellipses can be typical of the amateur woman writer who struggles to articulate her frustration whilst, at the same time, she fears what she really has to say. The final couplet is an artificial resolution: it sugars over the wish for death, the only conceivable escape route. In 'Woman At Home', Vere Arnot represents the entrapment of the married woman who is slave to her household. Again, the exclamation marks and cheery tone are thin disguises of female resentment at her repetitive routine; there were no positive models who could illustrate how fulfilment may be achieved – only the question, 'but what –?'. The madwoman in the home uses the fictional construction of the poem to complain.

Further Reading

Paul Berry, *Testament of a Generation: The Journalism of Vera Brittain and Winifred Holtby*, London, Virago, 1985.

Lady Margaret Rhondda, *This Was My World*, London, Macmillan, 1933.

Stella Gibbons

Continuity

> Bankers at war
> That gold may rule
> Dim lives that should be free,
> Space circular,

5   And faith gone cool.
And Time a mystery . . .
But from some old and plain delights
No puzzles shall me sever:
Love's act could speak
10   When Greek met Greek:
Some joys are good for ever.

Rose in her bower
Of thorn and leaf
Growing through history
15   As sweet as brief
And for eternity.
Fishing in history's murmuring tarn
Whence echo ceases never
With thought for cast
20   I'll catch the past
And stay by it for ever.

Roses were old
And wit was salt
With Ulysses at sea
25   Long before gold
Made thought a fault
Heavy in mine and me.
Serene by rose and murmuring tarn
No banking laws can sever
30   My senses share
The warm Greek air
Sweet once, and so for ever.

6 April 1935

Freda C. Bond

After the War

'After the war,' they used to say, and pictured
Perhaps a holiday at Bournemouth, or
Joining a tennis club, or just existence
Where neither casualty lists nor air raids nor
5   Shortage of meats troubled suburban households,
And life went on as it had done before.

After the war: you may say it again, but never,
Never, live it again.

After the war: the green fields are upheaved;
10   A black morass has swallowed the pastures; the trees, bereaved
Of their green tracery, are blackened signposts
Pointing at nothing.
There is no noise of guns, the machines are silent
There is no noise at all but the voice of the breakers
15   Beating for ever on a wreck-strewn shore,
Along the misty coast from Spain to Russia,
Where nobody is living any more.

Spring follows spring without her flowery crown,
Stiff in the poisoned earth the seeds are numb,
20   The years are long before the first green shoot
Pushes from under the twisted girders lying
Where Westminster once stood; are long before the root
Of the rose puts forth a branch to wreathe the walls
And roofless choir of Saint Paul's.

25   The years are long; and the white cliffs of Dover
See boats of brown-skinned people coming over,
Small, brown-skinned people coming from Africa,
Northwards through France their fathers came, and found
Nobody living there, and these,
30   Avid as Alexander, have dared the narrow seas –
Hewing their way through the thicket, they climb
To the cliff-top, and plant a cross of wood,
Redeeming the isle from its pagan gods, and the sun
Sees, as it founders in the western waters.

2 November 1935

Freda C. Bond

Pity Wasted

So many pangs of the tender heart for those
Who work all day in city office or store,
Electric light their sun, their horizon a brick wall,
These do not feel the stir of the seasons, see
5   The green tide sweeping over the land or the fire
Of autumn burning the dusty remains of summer.

Their seasons are measured by changes in the menu
At the cosy Dining Rooms,
By the alternation
10   Of football pools and points for punters.

But where are the heart pangs for us,
Leisured suburban ladies, free to stand in the sun,
To withstand the shattering assaults of spring,
To feel life draining away with ebbing summer,
15   To know the angry tug of autumn winds?
Every dart of light from the sequin leaves of spring
Pierces our armour, billows of blue air surging
Between clipped hedges raise us in pluming crests,
As they would carry us – whither? We do not know.
20   The hairdresser at eleven, bridge at half-past three,
Prevents us from keeping our appointment with life.

Pity for us: as for those other ones,
In the protective arrest of the city, eyes mercifully blind
To the immensity of wealth they cannot use,
25   I think you need not pity them so much,
Perhaps you need not pity them at all.

22 July 1939

Evelyn Poole

Last Prayer

The time has now gone by
For extravagant demand:
For one to love me till I die –
And the same one understand!

5   I would as soon lay claim
To a comet as to gold;
Ask freedom, gladness, travel, fame?
Not mine to make so bold.

Even to crave some peace
10   At the end, I would not dare –
Much less anticipate release
While I have strength to bear.

No: I can still endure

And neither rave nor weep,
15   If only this last thing be sure:
At the end of each day, sleep!

21 February 1932

Vere Arnot

Woman at Home

They come in,
And they go out
Incessantly! Incessantly!
And to the woman at home they have
5   No purpose! no purpose!

In and out,
Round and round,
Upstairs and down,
Banging doors as they go
10   Incessantly! Incessantly
And only the woman at home sees in all this
No purpose! no purpose!

But they can't keep going on,
As they do,
15   Incessantly! Incessantly!
Not without her:
She is their bread, their staff –
She makes their food.
Meals! They are nothing!
20   Hour preparing; in
A few moments forgotten.
To them she is but a 'muddle', having
No purpose! no purpose!
All day and every day,

25   Meals! meals!
'Come on, Mum, with the soup,
I've got to be there by eight sharp.'
'Coming to the dressmaker's, Mum?
I've got to be there by seven?'
30   'Granny, darling, are you going to put me to bed?'

Yet to-night she could drown them all;

Herself too:
What matters it when their end comes?
Round and round,
35 In and out
Incessantly! Incessantly!
All their lives will be this:
Why repeat the 'round' so often? with
No purpose! no purpose!

40 Is there not one side of her nature repressed?
Has she not longed, ached, craved for something for years?
Truth is: other minds have subjected hers
Incessantly! Incessantly!
Vainly has she striven (alas! in dreams) for release.
45 Will she get it – one day?
Her hand trembles as she carries the soup . . .

Ah! she is vain; she is sick;
She has always wanted to achieve
Something! Something!
50 But what –?
Why, something direct, with design;
Not that which goes round and round,
In and out, and back again with
No purpose! no purpose!
55 Oh! She is half-mad tonight,
The woman at home!

11 July 1936

Notes

1 Vera Brittain, *Testament of Experience: An Autobiographical Story of the Years 1925–1950*, London, Virago, 1979, p. 44.
2 'The University Idea', by Vera Brittain, 28 February 1931, p. 243.
3 'Oxford Union Divorce Debate', 12 December 1936, p. 1775.
4 E.M. Delafield is the pseudonym of Elizabeth Dashwood, née Edmée de la Pasture, 1890–1943, novelist and journalist, who is best known for her *Diary of a Provincial Lady* (1931).
5 Stella Gibbons, *The Mountain Beast and Other Poems*, 1931; *The Priestess and Other Poems*, 1934; *The Lowland Venus and Other Poems*, 1938; *Collected Poems*, 1951; all published by London, Longman.

Bibliography

Anthologies – Women's Poetry

ADCOCK, FLEUR, ed., *The Faber Book of 20th Century Women's Poetry*, London, Faber, 1987.

BERNIKOW, LOUISE, ed., *The World Split Open: Four Centuries of English and American Women Poets 1552–1950*, New York, Vintage Books, 1974; London, The Women's Press, 1979.

COSMAN, CAROL; KEEFE, JOAN; WEAVER, KATHLEEN, eds, *The Penguin Book of Women Poets*, Harmondsworth, Penguin, 1978.

COUZYN, JENI, ed., *The Bloodaxe Book of Contemporary Women Poets*, Newcastle upon Tyne, Bloodaxe Books, 1985.

PRITCHARD, R.E., ed., *Poetry by English Women: Elizabethan to Victorian*, Manchester, Carcanet, 1990.

REILLY, CATHERINE, ed., *Scars upon my Heart: Women's Poetry and Verse of the First World War*, London, Virago, 1981.

——, ed., *Chaos of the Night*, London, Virago, 1984.

SCOTT, DIANA, ed., *Bread and Roses: Women's Poetry of the 19th and 20th Centuries*, London, Virago, 1982.

Anthologies – General

ALLOTT, KENNETH, ed., *The Penguin Book of Contemporary Verse*, Harmondsworth, Penguin, 1950.

AUDEN W.H. ed., *The Oxford Book of Light Verse*, Oxford, Oxford University Press, 1939.

CUNNINGHAM, VALENTINE, ed., *The Penguin Book of Spanish Civil War Verse*, Harmondsworth, Penguin, 1980.

DAY-LEWIS, C; STRONG, L.A.G., eds, *A New Anthology of Modern Verse 1920–40*, London, Methuen, 1941.

GRIGSON, GEOFFREY, ed., *New Verse: an Anthology*, London, Faber, 1939.

——, *Poetry of the Present: An Anthology of the Thirties and After*, London, Phoenix House, 1949.

LEHMANN, JOHN, ed., *Poems from New Writing*, London, Lehmann, 1946.

MONRO, ALIDA AND HAROLD, eds, *Recent Poetry 1923–1933*, London, Gerald Howe & Co., The Poetry Bookshop, 1933.

MONRO, HAROLD, ed., *Twentieth Century Poetry 1929–1932*, revised and enlarged by Alida Monro, London, Chatto & Windus, 1933.

MOULT, THOMAS, ed., *Best Poetry*, London, Jonathan Cape, annual publication, vols 1930–9.

MURPHY, GWENDOLEN, ed., *The Modern Poet: An Anthology*, London, Sidgwick & Jackson, 1938.

RIDLER, ANNE, ed., *The Little Book of Modern Verse*, London, Faber, 1941.

ROBERTS, DENYS KILHAM; GOULD, GERALD; LEHMANN, JOHN, eds, *The Year's Poetry*, London, The Bodley Head, annual publication, 1934–8.

ROBERTS, MICHAEL, ed., *The Faber Book of Modern Verse*, London, Faber, 1936; revised edition with supplement by Anne Ridler, 1951.

——, *New Country, Prose and Poetry by the Authors of 'New Signatures'*, London, Hogarth Press, 1933.

RODWAY, ALLAN, ed., *Poets of the 1930s*, London, Longman, 1967.

SKELTON, ROBIN, ed., *Poetry of the Thirties*, Harmondsworth, Penguin, 1964.

SMITH, JANET ADAM, ed., *Poems of Tomorrow*, London, Chatto & Windus, 1935.

SPENDER, STEPHEN; LEHMANN, JOHN, eds, *Poems for Spain*, London, The Hogarth Press, 1939.

YEATS, W.B., ed., *The Oxford Book of Modern Verse 1892–1935*, Oxford, Oxford University Press, 1936.

Periodicals of the Period

Contemporary Poetry and Prose, ed. Roger Roughton, May 1936–Autumn 1937, London, Frank Cass, 1968.

The Criterion, ed. T.S. Eliot, vols viii–xviii, 1929–39, London, Faber, 1967.

Horizon, ed. Cyril Conolly, 1940–, vols 1–4, 1940–41, USA, Johnson Reprint Corporation, 1966.

Left Review, eds Montagu Slater, Amabel Williams, T.H. Wintringham, vols 1–3, London, Collets Bookshop, 1934–38.

The Listener, 1929–, London, British Broadcasting Corporation, 1929–.

New Statesman and Nation, London, The Statesman and Nation Publishing Company Ltd, 1931–.

New Verse, ed. Geoffrey Grigson, 1933–39, New York, Klauss Reprint Corporation, 1966.

New Writing, ed. John Lehmann, London, Lawrence & Wishart, 1936–39.

New Writing, New Series, eds John Lehmann, Christopher Isherwood, Stephen Spender, London, Lawrence & Wishart, 1938–39.

New Oxford Poetry, ed. A.W. Sandford, Oxford, Blackwell, 1936–37.

Oxford Poetry, ed. Richard Goodman, Oxford, Blackwell, 1929–32.

Poetry Review, London, The Poetry Society, 1909–.

Scrutiny, A Quarterly Review, eds D.W. Harding, L.C. Knights, F.R. Leavis, Denys Thompson, Cambridge, Cambridge University Press, 1932–39.

Time and Tide, Cheshire, Europress Limited, 1920–76.

Twentieth Century Verse, ed. Julian Symons, 1937–39, New York, Krauss Reprint Corporation, 1966.

Secondary Works

ALEXANDER, SALLY; FYRTH, JIM, eds, *Women's Voices from the Spanish Civil War*, London, Lawrence & Wishart, 1991.

BLAIN, VIRGINIA; CLEMENTS, PAULINA; GRUNDY, ISOBEL, eds, *A Feminist Companion to English Literature*, London, Batsford, 1990.

BRADBROOK, MURIEL, *Women and Literature 1979–1982: Collected Papers of Muriel Bradbrook*, Sussex, Harvester, 1982.

BRITTAIN, VERA, *Testament of Experience: An Autobiographical Story of the Years 1925–1950*, London, Virago, 1979.

——, *Testament of Friendship*, London, Virago, 1980.

BROE, MARY LYNN; INGRAM, ANGELA, eds, *Women's Writing in Exile*, Chapel Hill, University of North Carolina Press, 1989.

CAESAR, ADRIAN, *Dividing Lines: Poetry, Class and Ideology in the 1930s*, Manchester, Manchester University Press, 1991.

CARTER, RONALD, ed., *Thirties Poets: 'The Auden Group'*, London, Macmillan, 1984.

CUNNINGHAM, VALENTINE, *British Writers of the Thirties*, Oxford, Oxford University Press, 1988.

DE SOLA PINTO, VIVIAN, *Crisis in English Poetry*, London, Hutchinson, 1951.

HYNES, SAMUEL, *The Auden Generation: Literature and Politics in England in the 1930s*, London, The Bodley Head, 1979.

LEAVIS, F.R., *New Bearings in English Poetry*, London, Chatto & Windus, 1932.

LIGHT, ALISON, *Forever England: Femininity, Literature and Conservatism Between the Wars*, London, Routledge, 1991.

LUCAS, JOHN, ed., *The 1930s: A Challenge to Orthodoxy*, Sussex, Harvester; New York, Harper & Row, 1978.

MAXWELL, D.E.S., *Poetry of the Thirties*, London, Routledge & Kegan Paul, 1969.

MONRO, HAROLD, *Some Contemporary Poets*, London, Simpkins & Marshall, 1920.

PRESS, JOHN, *A Map of English Verse*, Oxford, Oxford University Press, 1969.

SCHMIDT, MICHAEL, *Introduction to 50 Modern British Poets*, London, Pan, 1979.

SCOTT, BONNIE KIME, ed., *The Gender of Modernism*, Bloomington, Indiana University Press, 1990.

SPENDER, DALE, *Women of Ideas and What Men Have Done to Them: From A. Behn to A. Rich*, London, Ark, 1983.

SPENDER, STEPHEN, *The Thirties and After: Poetry, Politics, People 1933–1975*, London, Collins/Fontana, 1978.

——, *World Within World: The Autobiography of Stephen Spender*, London, Hamish Hamilton, 1951; London, Faber, 1990.

SYMONS, JULIAN, *The Thirties: A Dream Revolved*, (London, The Cresset Press, 1960) London, Faber, 1975.

——, *Makers of the New: The Revolution in Literature 1912–1939*, London, André Deutsch, 1987.

——, *The Thirties and The Nineties*, Manchester, Carcanet, 1990.

TOLLEY, A.T., *The Poetry of the Thirties*, London, Gollancz, 1975.

TYLEE, CLAIRE, *The Great War and Women's Consciousness: Images of Militarism and Womanhood in Women's Writings 1914–1964*, London, Macmillan, 1990.

UNTERMEYER, LOUIS, *Modern British Poetry*, New York, Harcourt, 1925.

WOOLF, VIRGINIA, *A Room of One's Own*, London, Hogarth, 1929; London, Granada, 1977.

——, *A Woman's Essays*, Harmondsworth, Penguin, 1992.

Feminist Poetry Criticism

CAMERON, DEBORAH, *Feminism and Linguistic Theory*, Basingstoke, Macmillan, 1992.

GILBERT, SANDRA; GUBAR, SUSAN, eds, *Shakespeare's Sisters: Feminist Essays On Women Poets*, Bloomington, Indiana University Press, 1979.

MINOGUE, SALLY, ed., *Problems for Feminist Criticism*, London, Routledge, 1990.

MONTEFIORE, JAN, *Feminism and Poetry: Language, Experience, Identity in Women's Writing*, London, Pandora, 1987, revised 1994.

MONTEITH, MOIRA, ed., *Women's Writing: A Challenge to Theory*, Sussex, Harvester, 1986.

OLSEN, TILLIE, *Silences: How to Suppress Women's Writing*, London, The Women's Press, 1984.

OSTRIKER, ALICIA, *Stealing the Language: The Emergence of Women's Poetry in America*, London, The Women's Press, 1987.

RICH, ADRIENNE, *Blood, Bread and Poetry: Selected Prose 1979–1985*, London, Virago, 1987.

YORKE, LIZ, *Impertinent Voices: Subversive Strategies in Contemporary Women's Poetry*, London, Routledge, 1991.